PIRENE'S FOUNTAIN

Pirene's Fountain

Editor-in-Chief	*Lark Vernon Timmons*
Editors	*Mark McKay*
	Elizabeth Nichols
Managing Editor	*Steve Asmussen*
Associate Editors	*Royce Hamel*
	Paul Kim
Publisher & Editor	*Ami Kaye*

Pirene's Fountain: A Journal of Poetry
Volume 7, Issue 15
Copyright © 2014 Pirene's Fountain
Paperback ISSN 2331-1096

Design, Layout, and Cover Design: Steven Asmussen
Copyediting: Elizabeth Nichols
Cover Artist: Tracy McQueen

All rights reserved: except for the purpose of quoting brief passages for review, no part of this book may be reproduced or transmitted in any form or by any means, electronic or mechanical, including photocopying, recording, or by any information storage and retrieval system, without permission in writing from the publisher.

Glass Lyre Press, LLC
P.O. Box 2693
Glenview, IL 60025

www.GlassLyrePress.com

Pirene's Fountain

Volume 7, Issue 15

Fall, 2014

Dear Readers,

What a pleasure it is to welcome you to the inaugural print edition of *Pirene's Fountain*!

For nearly a decade it has been our privilege to bring *PF* to you as an online magazine; now largely due to our loyal readership, valued contributors, and the establishment of Glass Lyre Press, our vision to provide both print and online versions of our poetry journal has become a reality.

Looking forward, print issues of *Pirene's Fountain* are planned for annual publication each fall, followed shortly thereafter by an online version. Please visit GlassLyrePress.com and PirenesFountain.com for ordering information and submission guidelines. In addition, be advised ad space is available to interested parties.

Our special first print edition's cover and design concept are the creative vision of Tracy McQueen and Steve Asmussen, and we are honored to showcase and interview two talented and well respected poets, Jon Tribble and Melissa Studdard and FYI—next fall's showcases will feature noted poets, Allison Joseph and Lois P. Jones.

It is our pleasure to congratulate the 2013 Kithara Book Prize winner, Jeffrey C. Alfier for his book, *Idyll for a Vanishing River*, and 2014 Lyrebird Award winner, Connie Post for *Floodwater*, both from Glass Lyre Press.

In closing, valued newcomers, loyal readers, writers, artists, all—we hope you'll enjoy perusing the poetry on Pirene's crisp new pages in a way that leaves your copy comfortably dog-eared.

Lark Vernon Timmons
Editor-in-Chief
Pirene's Fountain

Vision is the true creative rhythm.
Robert Delaunay

Pirene's Fountain News & Events

2014 has been a busy year for *Pirene's Fountain*! After fourteen issues online, and the publication of two anthologies, we introduced an annual print version of the magazine; that issue was a year in the making! Additionally, writer and talk show host RJ Jeffreys interviewed publisher Ami Kaye on "The Write Step" radio show, and they spoke in depth about Glass Lyre Press and *Pirene's Fountain*. Then, in early spring, we attended the Association of Writers and Writing Programs (AWP) convention in Seattle.

AWP was an opportunity to reconnect with old friends and make new ones! We attended the beautiful Tiferet reading, and hosted a Pirene's Fountain/Glass Lyre Press event where many of our favorite poets read: Melissa Studdard, Donna Baier Stein, Amy King, Raul Sanchez, Connie Post, Kelly Cressio-Moeller, Diane Adair, Lori A. May and Hedy Habra. It was a special evening with great poetry! Here is a poem from one of our readers, Hedy Habra:

The Apple of Granada

Some say Eve handed a pomegranate to Adam, and it makes sense to me. How can the flesh of an apple compare to the bejeweled juicy garnets, the color of passion, hidden under its elastic pink skin tight as an undersized glove, a fruit withholding the power to doom and exile since the dawn of time. For a few irresistible seeds, didn't Persephone lose sight of the sun for months? I mean, think of the mystery hidden in its slippery gems, of the sweetness of the tongue sealing the union with the beloved in the Song of Songs. And I succumb, despite how messy it is to crack the fruits open, invade that hive, oblivious to the indelible droplets splattering the sink, reaching beyond the marble counter all over my arms and face, as my fingertips delicately remove its inner membranes, until the bowl is filled with shiny ruby red arils. I add a few drops of rose and orange blossom water, the way my mother did and my grandmother used to do and her mother before her.

reprinted from *Cumberland River Review*

In April, we hosted our first Live Lyre reading event at the Book Market at the Glen in Glenview, Illinois. Our readers included Marc Frazier, Diyva Rajan, Judith Tepfer, Nancy Wilson, Angela Narciso Torres, and Ralph Hamilton. Our special guests, Jon Tribble and Allison Joseph, came all the way from Carbondale, Illinois so that Allison could accept *RHINO's* Paladin Award the next day!

On September 27th, we celebrated the 100 Thousand Poets for Change global event. We folded origami cranes in remembrance of Sadako Sasaki, and to promote worldwide peace and sustainability. Our Live Lyre poets read their beautiful work, and we all connected through the diversity and power of poetry. At the mic were poets Gail Goepfert, Joan Colby, Jan Bottiglieri, Helen Degen Cohen, Bill Yarrow, Angela Narciso Torres, Virginia Bell, and Kathabela Wilson and her husband, Rick, who flew in from California. Kathabela's poetry was read with live flute accompaniment performed by her husband. Here is Kathabela's poem, "Flight from Yadz":

Flight from Yadz

the heart
has no name
no address

it only pretends
to be in
the body
it hides there
in the chest
curled up like a fetus

not knowing
how big
it can get

the heart
is always
ready to escape

it is not
man or woman
animal or bird

the heart
is always
waiting

tapping its foot
in the queue
from beginning to end
always
taking off or landing
applauding the pilot

First published in *Kyoto Journal*

2014 Poetry Contest Winners

Pirene's Fountain challenges readers and poets with online poetry contests to beckon the muse through inspiration, and to create a communal writing space that fosters an ongoing dialogue about poetry. This year, we hosted couplet, four line, haiku, and monostich contests. It is our privilege to present our 2014 contest winners below. For more information about Pirene's Fountain poetry contests, please visit us on Facebook!

Couplet Contest Winner — **Trish Lindsey Jaggers**

The rain lifts her skirt as she steps over our hill.
It is easy to believe the earth stands still.

◇

Four Line Contest Winner — **Kelly Cressio-Moeller**

Irony, Explained

When your mother dies
the first person
you want to call
is her.

◇

Four Line Contest Winner — **Hedy Habra**

Resonance

People talk of chemistry, of fields of energy, of parallel universes. Some recount
at least ten dimensions in which so much could be recovered...
But what of resonance, when one system is set in motion by the vibrations of another,
when people or strings tremble like two blue flames bent in the same direction?

Haiku Contest Winner — **Raymond Gibson**

DEPTH

Verbs streaming among
objects, how light
bathes a figure to shadow.

◇

Monostich Contest Winner - **Hedy Habra**

Every night is a canvas on which I reinvent a fabled version of you.

2014 Pushcart Prize and Best of the Net Nominations

Pirene's Fountain is pleased to nominate the following poems for the Pushcart Prize:

"The Medium Hand" — J.P. Dancing Bear
"The Landscape of Flight" — Lois P. Jones
"Entreaty" — Allison Joseph
"If the animals within you are quiet" — Rebecca Seiferle
"Feather — Angela" Narciso Torres
"The Scarab's Track" — Jon Tribble

Pirene's Fountain also nominates the following poems for the 2014 *Best of the Net Anthology*:

"Of Departure" — Walter Bjorkman
"This is What the Farmer Knows" — Lisa Cihlar
"Weather Vane II" — Joan Colby
"In Shadows of Cathedrals" — Lori Desrosiers
"Seeded" — Carol Lynn Grellas
"They Who See in the Dark" — Melissa Studdard

We thank all our nominees for sharing their very fine work with us, and wish them the best of luck!

2014 Liakoura Prize

Pirene's Fountain awards the Liakoura Prize to a poet with exceptional, and impactful, work. Poems are selected from the current issue by the *Pirene's Fountain* team of editors, and then sent blind to an outsider editor, who then chooses the winner.

Liakoura is the modern name of Mount Parnasssus, the home of the muses, in Greece. Specifically, Liakoura is where the mythical Pirene's fountain is located near Delphi. Due to its proximity to the wellspring of the muses, Liakoura is also broadly defined as a collection of poetry, the world of poetry and/or poets, or any active poetic or artistic space.

The *Pirene's Fountain* editors nominated the following poems for the 2014 Liakoura Prize Award:

"With(out) Him" — Ralph Hamilton
"Letter of Resignation" — Lissa Kiernan
"Bach's Little Anna Magdalena Book" — Ken Meisel
"Mapping" — Cindy Rinne
"The Animal in My Purse" — Maria Terrone
"The Weight of Air" — Pui Ying Wong.

This year's winner has been selected by Jessamyn Smyth. **Jessamyn Smyth** is the founding Director of the new international Quest Writer's Conference, which launches in June of 2015 with a stellar first faculty of warm, generous, and brilliant teacher-writers including Alicia Ostriker, Joy Harjo, Gregory Orr, Oliver de la Paz, and Rebecca Brown. www.questu.ca/quest_writers_conference.

Jessamyn was the founder, creator, and Editor in Chief of the literary & arts journal *Tupelo Quarterly*. Her chapbook *Kitsune* was a winner in the New Women's Voices Series of Finishing Line Press (2013), and will soon be followed by two more Trickster cycles. Her short story "A More Perfect Union" from *American Letters and Commentary* Issue 17 (November 2005) was selected as one of the "100 Distinguished Stories of 2005" by Best American Short Stories 2006. She was a recent finalist for both the Living Earth Nonfiction Prize of *Blue Lyra Review* (2014) and the Neil Shepard Prize of *Green Mountains Review* (2013). Her poetry, short stories, and prose appears in *The Taos Journal of International Poetry and Prose, Red Rock Review, Nth Position, Naugatuck River Review, Cezanne's Carrot, MiCrow/Full of Crow, Abalone Moon, Qarrtsiluni, The Montucky Review, Meat for Tea, Wingbeats: Exercises and Practice in Poetry*, and other journals and anthologies. Her plays have been produced by Arena Civic Theater, Naked Theater, The Paul Alexander Gallery, The Country Players, and The Shea Theater Festival of New Work. Jessamyn is a recipient of a 2010-2011 Welcome Hill Fellowship, a 2007 recipient of an artist's grant from The Vermont Community Foundation, and a 2004 special grant recipient of the Bread Loaf Writer's Conference. She is currently visiting faculty in Humanities at Quest University in British Columbia, and has taught at The University of Massachusetts, Amherst in The Commonwealth Honors College, Middlebury College, The University of Pennsylvania's Writer's Conference, and several other schools throughout New England.

Pirene's Fountain
presents the 2014 Liakoura Prize winner:

Maria Terrone
for
"The Animal in my Purse"

"The Animal in my Purse" can be found on page 163 of this issue.

Contents

Poetry

Jeffrey Alfier
- Red Bank Winterscape — 24
- Sonoran Sidewinder — 25

Francesca Bell
- Across God's Table — 26

Laboni Bhattacharya
- body — 27

Laurie Byro
- Angeli del Fango — 28
- Oracle — 29
- Silver Apples — 30

Hélène Cardona
- At My Funeral — 32
- Woodwork — 33

Kelly Cherry
- Jokes — 34
- Curiosity — 35

Lisa J. Cihlar
- The Color of Infidelity is Orange — 37
- Before the Next Ice Age — 38
- She Spoke of Plowing the Back Forty — 39

Tobi Cogswell
- On the Perimeter of the Packard Plant — 40

Joan Colby
- The Japanese Gardens — 41
- Incantations — 43

Rachel Abramson Dacus
- Love Is in the Air — 44
- Standing in the Shadows of Love — 45

J.P. Dancing Bear
- HC SVNT DRACONES — 46
- The Deepest Blues — 47
- The Medium Hand — 48
- The Ascent to Nothing — 49
- Dwindle — 50

Peggy Dobreer
    The Dazzling   51

Bruce Louis Dodson
    Bushido Steel   52

Howard Faerstein
    Spaghetti & Meatballs   53
    [What a Sunday!]   55

Ricky Garni
    The Last First Date   56

Ralph Hamilton
    Safari   57
    Wait   59
    With(out) Him   61

David M. Harris
    Things Dogs Chew   62

Meg Harris
    Snake   63

Melinda B Hipple
    Cataracts   65
    Guernica   66

Jane Hirshfield
    Zero Plus Anything Is A World   67
    Ordinary Rain. Every Leaf Is Wet.   69
    I Cast My Hook, I Decide To Make Peace   70
    Mop Without Stick   72

Cin Hochman
    Legs   73
    E.R.   74
    Self-Referential   75
    Insomnia   77

Claire Ibarra
    Silk Threads   78

RJ Jeffreys
    The Rain   80
    Down To The Boats   81

Cambria Jones
    Here I Am at Age Fifteen   82
    Paean   83

Lois P. Jones
- The Landscape of Flight — 84
- In Between Lives — 87
- To the Scarlet Tanager — 88
- The Cobb - Lyme Regis — 89

Allison Joseph
- A Ballad for Lucille, Whom I Met on the Shuttle Home — 92
- Entreaty — 94
- Accident — 95

Winnie Khaw
- I did not know — 96
- Like glaze on pottery — 97

Robert S. King
- The Painted Forest — 98
- Stubborn Leaf — 100
- The Invisible Man Works the System — 101

Lissa Kiernan
- Letter of Resignation — 102
- Dear Leonora, — 103
- Fetish — 104

Usha Kishore
- Mermaid - On Hanuman — 106

Laurie Kolp
- The Mortician — 109

Victoria Korth
- Tree of My Heart — 110

W.F. Lantry
- Lessons — 111
- San Dieguito River — 112

Rustin Larson
- The Curse — 113
- Bumble — 114
- The Artist — 115

Ann Neuser Lederer
- Increasingly Speaking of Rain — 116

Stephen Linsteadt
- Saint-Rémy de Provence — 117

Dennis Maloney
  Crossing the Yangtze 118
Alexandra Martin
  Finished Business 119
  Blank Verse 120
Matt McGee
  Blue 121
Ken Meisel
  Bach's Little Anna Magdalena Book 122
  My Wife & I 124
B.Z. Niditch
  Los Angeles Eyes 125
Richard King Perkins II
  Satan's Antlers 127
Anne Elezabeth Pluto
  Tom O'Bedlam in the Garden of Eden 128
Brie Quartin
  The Roseate Scarf 129
Cindy Rinne
  dark days 130
  mapping 131
  Fragments 132
  The Road 133
Mary Kay Rummel
  Reading Zagajewski in Prague 134
Peter L. Scacco
  Mare tentaculorum 135
Rebecca Seiferle
  Syllabus 136
  Love has no children of its own 138
  she thinks of her hands 140
  Being Born at Any Hour 142
  If the animals within you are quiet, 143
LeRoy N. Sorenson
  Dusk Going Home 145
  The Armstrong Boys 146
  Among the Survivors 147

Ron Starbuck
    Running With Wolves   149
    Wizard & Whiteface Clown *(Zen Priest)*   *150*

Donna Baier Stein
    Roget's Thesaurus   153

Robert Strickland
    Before Counting the Cost He Follows Her
        to the End of the Road   156
    Passage   157

Melissa Studdard
    We Are the Universe   158

Tim Suermondt
    Oran   159
    Keeping Up   160
    The Circumference Of The World   161

Maria Terrone
    Consolation   162
    The Animal In My Purse   163

Charles Thielman
    Solitude   164
    A Painting, An Early Morning Walk,
        and All the People   165

Angela Narciso Torres
    Feather   166
    Garden, End Of Summer   167
    August Moon   168

Jon Tribble
    The Scarab's Tracks   169

Kenneth Weene
    Acero   171

Helen Wickes
    Mountain Lake, September   172
    Summer's Drift   173

Pui Ying Wong
    For The Hour   174
    The Weight Of Air   175
    In Summer's Evening   176

Features & Interviews

Melissa Studdard: Radio Host with Spirit and Poetry to Share — 180
In Conversation with Poet and Author Melissa Studdard — 190
Jon Charles Tribble: Academician with an Editor's Eye — 194
In Conversation with Professor and Poet Jon Tribble — 210

Reviews

A Girl Goes into the Woods — 221
Blood Orange — 225
Eye to Eye — 228
In Both Hands — 232
Moon Over Zabriskie — 236
On Manannan's Isle — 240
Six Weeks to Yehidah — 244
The Gathering Light at San Cataldo — 246
The Map of What Happened — 249
Woman in Metaphor — 253
Developing a Photograph of God — 257

Publication Credits — 259

Contributor Notes — 262

Advertisements — 281

POETRY

Red Bank Winterscape

Jeffrey Alfier

Wind was heavy in the trees last night.
It played at will through the windows and bricks

of this aging house, found its own way in,
like the angel at Pharaoh's door. Today in town,

dustgray clouds evoke the billowed breakers
of a running sea. A homeless man I've always seen

on my visits home sentinels a street corner
he never abandons. I slipped him two bucks.

He touched my face as a child might.
Tonight, through bedroom doors,

I'll hear my father sigh uncertainly in his sleep,
muttering off-key. At first light, his hands will cup

icy cold from the bathroom faucet to his face.
Clouds will break above the wet silence of snow.

Sonoran Sidewinder

Jeffrey Alfier

His hide's a hint of driftwood smoke
coasting over the stones of a dead river.

Unleashed in the sun's wake, his body
wades over ground in oblique loops

to ferry the boiling heat away,
surety of traction in a series of J's –

recursive, slurred tracings, as if
inscribed by a sun-stroked traveler

desperate to beseech God solely
by the first letter of 'Jehovah.'

At midday, the curved vector
of his venom slumbers beneath

the surface of loose, boiling sand,
or in shaded havens under creosote.

Night hunter, he will glide
with the grace of molten silver,

uncoil in the mineral gaze of desert,
all his sunsets the blood of light.

Across God's Table

— For H Francesca Bell

I haven't stopped loving you,
man doing time for murder—
one year for each of the sixteen times
your knife rent another man's flesh.
Hard time that won't restart
the delicate engine of his life.
Tattoos cover the body you've built here,
armor you harden into every day.
Your eyes are guarded,
face worn out by the penitentiary—
but we sat across the table as children,
good food sticking in my throat
as your father thrust his fingers
into your afro, jerking us all to attention.
Sometimes in summer they let you out
of your room to play. I chased you
and chased you, your body a dark streak
crossing the lawn. Now, on trips outside,
chains hang from legs you've made
strong enough to hold what you carry.
You are dark as chocolate is dark:
bitterness beneath a glossy sheen.
I look at your grown man's face,
eyes shining darkly at me,
and the boy grins back.
Catch me catch me if you can—
but I was a skinny white girl,
never that fast.

body

Laboni Bhattacharya

I want to unzip my skin
step out of my flesh
and look at myself
for the very first time

Or perhaps stay in
reach down my back
and pull out, itchy
stubs of bitten-off wings

And wake up
with my legs tangled
in a tail that looks and feels
like the missing piece of me

I want to strike a match
burn my old body up
and start all over again
this time do it right.

Angeli del Fango

Another for Mitchell Laurie Byro

Sometimes, the mud has taken me in. When you dig up
a tree, keep some soil around the roots. In time,

I stretch myself and I am my mother's mother. I am
an angel smoothing the white alabaster statues free

of grime. In time, I shall become all that you wanted:
a rickety Mucha poster floating down cobbled streets

that are filled with tears, a sparkling choir of angels,
dark ice air forming halos. I have forgotten my poems.

Sex and bread, my faults are common ones. Mud wrens rise
over the streets of Florence, the breath of a lonely God.

Oracle

Laurie Byro

When his spirit came to me from the North, spouting
nose-gays and jealousies, all those manly pursuits, I knew

I was in trouble . Consider the words he left "make a pledge, for
mischief is nigh." Then consider my dilemma. Mischief?

What bored Tower-Damsel wouldn't want that? To some, even
his words are illegitimate. I rave a little. It is his words, not vapors,

that intoxicate my senses. Heady I become from those old taunts:
long Vowels and short A's. "Tarantula, monsoon, antler":

I can bear it, if you can. Even the goats are mesmerized.
Let this be a lesson to all women and men who adore mortals

who have a way with words. We shall grow our hair long to stuff
up our ears. Sing: tra la, tra la. Let their gutturals be captured

into a potion-bottle we clamp down with a cork.
Once upon a time, a lavender vowel escaped and I was left pining

in a turret. I was left with goats and chickens that cluck and bray.
Fancy me, and my fine fashion sense; I've adorned

my hair with plumes. A warning: you mustn't let some randy-hoofed
mischief-man talk you into letting your hair down

permanently. No free man or woman wants to lose his way,
fall off the tower, take her first tumble.

Silver Apples

Der Apfel fallt nicht weit vom Stamm.
—German Proverb

Laurie Byro

I have worn you, a white chemise against
my numbness, when I lie down at night.
I am so bright in these dark hours, moths

hover over me, little ghosts attracted
to my shine. Daddy, you were mine.

I leave you. I leave the country, arrogant
in its stupidity, to rub pages of poems—
I inflame, a spark against a vein, I stumble

on cobblestones, long before I lose feeling
in my feet. In vineyards, I set fire to your picture,
watch your ears curl, your mouth, too full of noise.

I have chanted Dante Alighieri and watched us
become soot. There are Polish towns where peasants

wring out nappies. When I ask you where you came
from you don't know, but I think you were
born on the barn, like the Luna moth that hatched.

How green you glow against the red wood.
You enter my ears at night. Luminous engine,

you work and work and work. Arbeit
Macht Frei, you and I are a country
of farmers and serfs. I sop up your blood

with the brown bread my husband has baked
in his oven. You will fly back to me, sooty spirit

with green wings, eyes of a man of Arles.
Another circumstance, another year of wintering,
as I am summering now. Daddy, soon you will be

in a place I cannot touch. In Donegal, it is already night,
and I let the loose soil of us sift through my fingers.

All fathers tell lies, all writers are liars.
And at Yeats' grave, in the mossy town of Sligo,
cats stalk moths under a host of silver apples.

At My Funeral

Hélène Cardona

Nothing is born or perishes, but already existing things combine, then separate anew.
        —Anaxagoras

Somebody spoke at my funeral
but I wasn't dead.
People loved the eulogy,
couldn't get enough.
It wasn't sad.
Water flooded out of
nowhere, mingled with air
and the fluidity converted you from solid
to liquid to ether and back.
Cats sauntered in the condensation.
I remember looking for them.
Finding all the cats meant
there was no death.

Forthcoming from *Life in Suspension* (Salmon Poetry), first published in *From the Fishouse*

Woodwork

Hélène Cardona

If I could gather all the sadness of the world,
all the sadness inside me
into a gourd,
I'd shake it once in a while
and let it sing,
let it remind me of who I used to be,
bless it for what it taught me
and stare at it lovingly
for not seeping out of its container.

Forthcoming from *Life in Suspension* (Salmon Poetry), first published in *The Astonished Universe* (Red Hen Press)

Jokes

Kelly Cherry

When people laugh, they step inside themselves.
No longer are they on the outside, estranged
From their emotions and removed from that
Which is at the heart of all human hearts,
The fellowship of knowing what we know:
That each of us is single and alone
But all of us are blessed by company.

Yet he or she who makes the joke—the pun
Or witty observation or a story
With a punch line—stands apart, if only for a moment,
And perhaps enjoys the laughter and the triumph
But cannot fully share the fellowship.
What irony. To cause the thing and not
Embrace the freedom of unself-consciousness.

I think it better to give oneself over
To general glee than be a second-rate god,
Though I am glad such local gods exist
In books and at the dinner table, and truthfully
It's hard not to pity such cool cucumbers
Who keep their gifted heads while all around
The rest of us are laughing our heads off.

Curiosity

Kelly Cherry

I did not kill the cat.
I was not programmed for that.
My mission, should I accept,
NASA said, was "scoot and shoot."
I arrived on Mars intact
after charging through miles
of nowhere and air pressure
so low that it would rupture
a human and kill him more
or less instantly.
Now I am here, the one
moving thing among
such stillness I might be
an actor working alone
before a green screen
although the screen is red,
or reddish, or sandy red,
something like the Sahara,
this place called Gale Crater.
As instructed, I
photograph or collect
samples of what I find
to blast with laser pulses
then assess with my ChemCam,
but in profound darkness,
when I can get away
with it, I aim my sensors
at the sky, hoping to see
another one of me,
companion, colleague, someone
or something with which to share
at least a little of

the overwhelming time
that weighs me down and down.
The stars gaze back with no
sign of recognition.
If I could wave I would.
Surely, scientists
could have supplied me with tears
that I could shed to drown
this dreadful, debilitating
Loneliness. Am I
so alien? A stranger
in an even stranger land?

The Color of Infidelity is Orange

Lisa J. Cihlar

I am out of bed much too early,
the ground fog still floats over
the pastures and corn fields.

Corn weeps humidity,
adding to the commotion.
And crickets, grasshoppers,

katydids, sound both nearby
and far away. I can't remember
the lies I told you, so now I

must make up something new.
Affairs and abortions. Sucking
a crooked man until nothing

remained but a limp snail.
See, for just a second your heart
jumps wild until you remind

yourself that these are lies
and half-truths. That reaction
is what I am looking for.

Before the Next Ice Age

Lisa J. Cihlar

The girls used to stand in the garden at night fluorescing tomato hornworms with handheld black lights. Talemother let them wear white, flouncy, nightgowns. Dry soil cooled their feet and gave them shivers. The bed sheets became stained at the bottom end. Story-books from those days are now foxed where their fingers turned the pages. No one reads any more. It is too cold and dark. Talemother tells them stories by the fire. She remembers the before. The taste of tomatoes and delight of a worm popping green underfoot. Scrabble under the snow by the edge of the river and there is sometimes a bit of cress. It sounds enough like caress to be dangerous. The oldest daughter brushes the youngest daughter's hair just like they always did.

She Spoke of Plowing the Back Forty

Lisa J. Cihlar

A choir-wind claims my head today. Living on the edge of the driftless zone, this is the hard truth: ice moves slowly. A near lobe releases melt-water to slake my thirst. Another farmer has died of a broken heart. Another! That makes three and one is related to me. She told me of tilling the land where the black dirt turned up so many worms that the seagulls and robins veiled the tractor and she imagined she was a bride every spring. Sandhill cranes came after, pecking out seed corn so whole rows grew nothing but weeds. And what of the horses and mules that my next-door farmer had? They are in winter pasture down by the river, but who is going to take care of them now? Eggs are freezing under the chickens. They are on the way to becoming fossils. We feel lucky to find a perfect arrowhead turned up by the plow. In the winter farmer John practiced flint knapping. When it became winter all the time, he lost his need.

On the Perimeter of the Packard Plant

Corner of Frederick &
Bellevue, Detroit, MI

Tobi Cogswell

Cell block, tenement, Dresden,
the color of dead December sky.

Not one of a thousand panes intact.
Some shattered in by throwing arms and dares,

some crushed among the rubble
by boredom, distrust, defeat.

Cement, brick, the odd mallet made in Japan.
This is a funeral with no wake,

no drunken dirges of hope, just drunks.
Just graffiti. Half a boat not shaped

enough for shelter or pleasure.
This blank-eyed stare of a city defines

the word gray as ugly. Even a kiss of snow
offers no redemption for rust.

The Japanese Gardens

Joan Colby

Designed by Hoichi Kurisu. Thirty years
In the making. The winding paths
Lead to meditation pools
Where gold, silver and black Koi
Swerve to a sinuous music.

Waterfalls splash into ponds
Where the teahouse shelters
Beneath Scotch Pines rigged
With tension wires to distort
Into full-sized Bonsai trees.
In spring the needles are clipped, the bark
Roughened to expose its ruddy muscle.

A small isle for the master to burn
Incense to honor the ancestors. The boardwalks
Zigzag to forestall demons
Who can only travel in straight lines.

Everything is mastered and ordained.
Each miniature vista: perfect.
My father admired this aesthetic.
Brought us a young bonsai with directions
for its torment that I could not impose.

We rest upon a rough-hewn bench.
The leaves here are turning.
The poplars tremble whispering
Their alias. The sand raked
In crosshatch patterns. The ponds
Deepened so the Koi can overwinter.

The mallards depart
With the first frost. Every winter brings
The axe of ice. Every spring the crews
Remonstrate with acts of nature
Insisting beauty is artifice.

Incantations

Joan Colby

Twisted forest light compels
An utterance of druids
Blue as agony.

A magpie reveres
Its treasures,
Tinfoil, a copper coin.

Think of the brigandry
Of crows. Crazed speech
That etches glass.

How priests
Raise chalices full of
Dead language.

Women whisper behind
Onyx rings. They want to tell
Unspeakable things.

The cant of politicians
Paints the wall with duplicity
Cowering like a cat boys have stoned.

Sweet ejaculations sever
Years of burning. Come close, I'll
Show you what a spell is.

Love Is in the Air

Rachel Abramson Dacus

Eyes still closed without memory
of the world, birdsong fills me
with messages. They tell me to inhale
before I catch up to my brood
of woes and sag, to flow
with their diamond notes.

I'm not even in love
with anyone I can name,
though every name
sails the swell of my heartbeat,
carries a strange beloved in its boat.
It's in the air, every sight and every sound,
a feature in the face of that One.

Standing in the Shadows of Love

Rachel Abramson Dacus

I lie down with loss and its arms
tighten around me, a sweet vise.
I stroke its cheek. You are not alone, I say.
I take it out walking, down the road
of music piped into our ear.
Passing a maple's twittering, it grows
wings and lifts my feet off.

In the morning I braid its beard
into a tapestry of fathers, lovers,
friends, and cousins.
It opens to show me
golden, fringed pistils. It nuzzles
the depths of my heart.
By afternoon it wears a beautiful, aged face
I will never again see.
It hovers in the promise of touch.
It stands in the shadows,
luminous and green, a pregnant
sky's blue salt skin.
I will give you birth, I say.

HC SVNT DRACONES

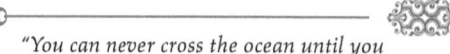

"You can never cross the ocean until you have the courage to lose sight of the shore."
—Christopher Columbus

J.P. Dancing Bear

We slip out, but later will claim to have been drawn or pulled,
we will blame all of the nautical gods, and a few thousand demons,
for whatever goes wrong or right depending on the penmanship
of the author. Parents will cite the damage of their children,
children the damaged love of their parents. We move away
not so much to explore, but to escape, to pray sometimes
that there is an edge to the flat earth. And to keep sailing
as careless as a cloud's mouthful of wind.

◇

It would be easy to believe we are not those ghosts crowding
into creaking boats, that we look all ways before crossing now.
We might even chuckle or laugh at what backward fears
what foolish beliefs were printed on the yellow crumble of maps.
Out here in the windless Sargasso Sea, it is hardest to admit
we brought an ocean of monsters with us—we always do.

The Deepest Blues

J.P. Dancing Bear

O tide and tiding, and always the back and forth froth of salt
and its taste on the wind, while I can hear the seabirds
calling out over the waves—have they come through
the front door left open? And even on calmer days
the ocean still displays its frightening power, still pulls
the living from their shores, draws them out
and away and into the deepest blues. All the while,
offering you some distant fin or tail of distraction.

I light another candle, the room darkening with sunset.
Salt and sand never fail to enter my eyes especially here,
at your vanishing point. I write another elegy on the tide's edge.
I think of you in your blue couch just drifting at the earth's curve.
I searched through all the beached shells I could find—
my ear to each, listening for the wave that might bring you back.

The Medium Hand

*after Charles Rain's
"The Magic Hand"*

J.P. Dancing Bear

What the hand knows best is to pose
In classic stances of labor and epiphany
So that the light divides the hand into two realms.
For the theater of the fingers tarot cards are deployed—
The Hanged Man and The Fool begin their seasonal dance.
Here the hand slights its own image, snapshot of the past,
Framed in a plaster backbone, learned, and alone
In a corner of a room, pouring over old schematics
And drawings of church steeples.
The hand fantasizes a fist into a shell into an egg,
And so gathers lovingly the spiraled feathers
Of raptors. What the hand vividly recalls
Is Cat's Cradle and wearing knots of memory.
The hand stands dramatic, looking outward—
A soothsayer, fingers all a swagger, the beating palm-
Heart with its smooth life lines.
Lifting The Devil card like a throwing star,
The shadow from the wrist, diving out over the edge
Of this realm. Voiceless, it invents no signal or dance,
it chants no incantation, recites no prayer. It hears
no evidence and witnesses no event. What the hand
Feels is all it ever knows—in every moment
it is both grasping and letting go.

The Ascent to Nothing

J.P. Dancing Bear

I sit upon the remnants of aspirations—
those desires to rise above the yellowing plains
of this life. I've lived building ladders that went
only so far before a rung broke or I ran
out of rails. Once I hitched a line to the moon
but only pulled it down. Once I stood atop
an antelope that could not leap
with our combined weight. Once I started
a shell-shock war but bombs could not lift the economy
of the soul to flight, even as the jets returned home.
The clouds in my sky ran together like smoke,
they did not break into free animal spirits.
Oh sure, I fancied myself a centaur once,
but I lost most of my hooves and my head
leapt like laundry in the wind.

Dwindle

J.P. Dancing Bear

I make plans for a September harvest
of the close ball of soil I call my earth—
all the things to put on my plate by way
of the rake and the net and the snare.
I flush out the rat and the hare and snake—
set traps to stave any return
to the root and the leaf and fruit.
I've spent all spring and summer nurturing
the plants, tending the lanes of crops;
pretending each blister and sweat and tear,
a rain I didn't carry in buckets for miles.
In the daylight heat-spells I raved,
while at night sat staring at the near-empty
pan reciting the best winter tales.
Soon it would be time to pick then rest
from working the ever smaller and small earth.

The Dazzling

after "Die Erblindende"
by Ranier Maria Rilke

Peggy Dobreer

It's the way we are changed
whenever sipping tea. Who will be

served first, diving into an unknown
cup? There is so little warning

when change catches hold. Laughter
comes—sometimes not. Is it a crime,

the way we smile or raise ourselves
to speak? How can we walk toward

birth without terror? Behavior imagines
it so. We want to sing loud into dawn.

But we walk so far behind the others,
eyes lit up like the surface of a sunlit pond

from which we soon may drink. The shadow
turns slowly, will not survive another night.

And here with a single gesture, we see
that we can fly.

Bushido Steel

Bruce Louis Dodson

Only the winter wind surrounds me
Soldiers do not come to look for death
Inside this cave
My sword's calligraphy is perfect
Brush of steel
Red ink on white snow.

Spaghetti & Meatballs

Howard Faerstein

Since there have only been two brief encounters with aliens
I've had no chance to serve them my specialty,
spaghetti & meatballs.
I did once cook the dish for a reunion,
though since dad & new wife arrived five hours late
& I forgot my brothers don't speak to each other
the dinner didn't amount to much.
I didn't bother showing them the half-dead catalpa
flowering eighteen springs in a row
that Lou, ex-brother-in-law, early on advised me to cut down.
I never made spaghetti & meatballs for his family.
But I did for old, dear friends just before leaving the East
& once for my son-in-law's French parents
gazing on Brooklyn for the first time
& then last night for new friends in Santa Fe
in our house surrounded by fruiting apricot trees.
Always from a "sixty minute" recipe,
always with garlic bread, salad & red wine.

Both times the aliens shifted the trailhead.
First, in the hills of Western Massachusetts
where a sugar maple,
prophesied to topple only if a hurricane hit,
towered in view of the front window.
& after the hurricane hit I prepared spaghetti & meatballs
for my second wife's son.
The next incident involved hiding the gate
leading out of the Pecos Wilderness after a four hour hike.
Aliens are quite crafty in never leaving clues or breadcrumbs
which along with oregano, hot pepper, rosemary & marjoram
are a key ingredient of the meatballs.

My mom used to say she wanted normal boys
then she kept the three of us in a room with two windows.

[What a Sunday!]

Howard Faerstein

What a Sunday! After a night's loopy sleep
you've no remembrance of how dreams ransacked
your body other than this:
a young couple in formal dress emerges from deep water
cradling an infant—
it must have been you,
impossibly dry:
you will spread just as aspen.
Or perhaps the offering still-born, their lament bringing an
irrevocable close.

Then day arrives with its echo of repetition
and emptiness as if nothing—
the mist and brown field,
the grey distant light,
evergreens rising behind phone lines, electric wires—
nothing can fill the imagination's absence—
blues booming on the radio
tea steeping on the oak table
wood fire setting the morning red hot.

The Last First Date

Ricky Garni

If the highway is a ribbon
what is it tied around?
More importantly,
what is the sky if not
old movies that you can
take pictures of?
But why take a picture
of an old movie
speeding out of control
tied around a gift
that is to big to carry
to June's house with
a fresh bottle of wine?

Safari

Ralph Hamilton

Below a flat-roofed acacia
              with five-inch thorns, my son sticks me
     again,
          flicking ticks
from my back with a giant porcupine quill.
                      Before breakfast
   still, we watch the veldt lengthen,
                            shift—filling
            with dust and herds
     and hunger.

He counts, "Fifteen!"

I tell him about the puff adder
               found at dawn this morning,
    its head
                     as big as his grandfather's fist,
   a finger's width from my left foot:

  how the Masai guide
               did a double salchow,
    rifle in one hand, me
                   in the other,
  how the clay was red ocher.

My son loses count after eighty-four ticks,
      laughing hard
             with hyenas across the gorge.

It frightens me,
        my love for this boy:
                I don't know how
                        to protect myself
                  from him.
      I reach around to pat his cheek—
                        he pulls away.

Gazelles
        scatter.
    I stare   at my hands:
        one,   the other—
                my father's hands.

Wait

for Retha Schlabach Ralph Hamilton

They don't care for us
                or wear coathanger haloes,

    they don't bear wings and dirt
                    clings to their feet.

        For flight alone

               never made a thing
holy. Yet sometimes

somehow
              in the chimney-flue space

      between soil and sky—air breaks
                                open—

and easy, unburdened
                    the moon escapes
        a pail of black water,

     a wing-rush of bees
             eclipses the sun,

                       and antelope leap
       leaving the ground
          on wind-borne limbs—

as if weight suspended,
                    the earthbound rise:

    Perhaps like clouds
           they cover us
       all, perhaps

     like rain
they return.

With(out) Him

Ralph Hamilton

In the yard outside my window is a blue rhinoceros, a blue rhinoceros afloat in my yard. Perhaps he's part whale, perhaps barracuda, the blue rhinoceros with eyes so small, set so far apart. I watch him all day, though he seems unaware. He lolls in the shallows on green velvet moss, on rockweed, sargassum, on plankton and dulse, the great blue brute in blue-gray shadows that ripple, that wave like large sea fans, like large sea fans in my backyard. He preys on my mind. Will he breach, will he spout, does he graze among coral, strain krill from the lawn, the blue rhinoceros in my velvet yard? I would stroke him and feed him if he would allow, might fondle his snout, I'd tickle wee ears that rise from his hump. It may be I love him. No doubt that's absurd. And yet I'm afraid of the blue brutal beast at home in my yard. Because if startled, he could capsize my house, could deflate my lungs with his horn, with hoof weight and his small-set eyes, the blue rhinoceros now backstroking my yard. Or else dive down deep, like a whale he might sound to the blue-black depths below bluestone and sod in my broad backyard. From there he might vanish, may very well vanish (and never return) from waves, from moss, from the vast callous reef engulfing my lot. Without him I'm lost. Like water, I breathe him. I drink him like air.

Things Dogs Chew

David M. Harris

Bones, of course,
and dog toys, especially
knots of rope or plastic
boneshapes infused with chicken.
The awful savor of your
shoes, until they learn better,
if they do. When they've been
abandoned while you go
out to dinner, or a movie:
books, or a favorite hat.
(How do they reach these?)
When you reappear: your hands
and fingers, with gentle,
joyous forgiveness.

Snake

Meg Harris

The large black rat-snake
which hunts along the top
of the cement block walls
in the ladies bunk
has molted again leaving
her intricate translucent
skin dangling above the card
room window.

I'm pretty certain she is why
I've not seen bats swooping
for insects in the stale night air
over my cot. And she is why
some afternoons I find
debris on my bed's pillow
unknown leavings cast down
from the wall's top when this
hunter passed above.

I saw her once
when I was showering
held up my fingertips
into the stream of water
letting it sluice my arms
and breasts. I remembered to look
up as I have every time I've showered
there since as a girl I happened
to do so and see
the eyes of a man staring at me.

The snake did not alarm
me, though showering I'd have
little defense were she to attack.
She brought the long heft of her body
through the rafters and moved with a noiseless
grace to her next capture of rat or mole.
All these years later I am competent
in the ways of danger. I know
which things ought to drag me from
my sleep.

Cataracts

Melinda B Hipple

The fog is gone
from eyes surgically new.
Without time to adjust, to grow
into awareness,
she becomes the child
born wholly sentient, dropped
into a new world of dazzling hues,
crisp edges, a granddaughter's beauty
fully revealed. She has no time to adapt
to the age of her own skin
even while the blue of her eyes
seems bluer looking in.

Guernica

*Oil on canvas, by Pablo
Picasso, 1937*

Melinda B Hipple

In this dance macabre,
a bull, a horse
close the distance
from horn to heart,
spill gray hope
upon Basque soil.

A beauteous brushstroke
no longer serves
to shake us
from the glorified gore
of broken blades
and severed limbs.

These dagger tongues scream
of shifting dimensions,
of space out of time,
of a dark aftermath
where we will ride the chaos
on our knees.

And we will ride
without surrender
for as long as Man finds honor
in the death of children.

Zero Plus Anything Is A World

Jane Hirshfield

Four less one is three.

Three less two is one.

One less three
is what, is who,
remains.

The first cell that learned to divide
learned to subtract.

Recipe:
add salt to hunger.

Recipe:
add time to trees.

Zero plus anything
is a world.

This one
and no other,
unhidden,
by each breath changed.

Recipe:
add death to life.

Recipe:
love without swerve what this will bring.

Sister, father, mother, husband, daughter.

Like a cello
forgiving one note as it goes,
then another.

Ordinary Rain. Every Leaf Is Wet.

Jane Hirshfield

The etching by Durer
of a dandelion amid grasses

its flowers

done with the first opening
not yet gone into the second

these too will finally bend toward the earth

exiles
writing letters
sent over the mountains by friendly horses and donkeys

I Cast My Hook, I Decide To Make Peace

Jane Hirshfield

The bee does not speak to me.
The whale does not speak to me.
The horse is silent.

History does not speak to me.
Arachne is only a spider.

Nothing says "you" if I offer "I,"
"I" if I proffer "you."

I would go
to the Counter of Complaining—

there was one,
a hut of new pine wood
at the base of the Yellow Mountains in China,
the door was open, a woman sat in the chair—

but nothing says "counter,"
nothing says "yellow" or "mountain."

Erased dust of the chalkboard, barnacle,
less sleep than bed—
what can I do, faceless, with no one to kiss or shout at?

I cast my hook, my vote against it,
I decide to make peace.

I declare this intention but nothing answers.
And so I put peace in a warm place, towel-covered, to proof,
then into an oven. I wait.
Peace is patient and undemanding, it *surpasseth*.

And the bulldozers move
from the palace of breaking to the places of building.
And the students return to their classes.
Tuna swim freely.
The sky hoists the flag of the sky.

All this in the space of a half-page, a little ink,
a small bite of hubris
sweetened with raisins and honey.

I begin to consider what I will make of tomorrow's speechless.

Mop Without Stick

Jane Hirshfield

I am on my knees again,
mop without stick,
over old fir trees turned into flooring.
A thought stood once in the middle,
near the cookstove, left heel and right heel.
Left hand and right hand, I wash around it.
Thought without handle,
thought without hands, without lemons or Serengeti.
One breath, another,
one corner of cotton in water wets the whole cloth.

Legs

Cin Hochman

Back when I was ether-eyed and doe-legged, back with my Buddha breaths and a little pastel heart, back with my unruly mop of wild wheat hair and unholy mess of wild thoughts, back when my home was the porcelain throne, back when I smelled like sea-spray and foam, back when I had a quick trigger tongue, back when I was not so wound up and not so wounded, back when I'd fall down on my sweet knees and say *god bless these moon-thin legs*, jackknifed and splayed, with no spider veins—my precious legs in assorted beds.

E.R.

Cin Hochman

None of my wounds are superficial. Burned fingers, bullet holes. Gash, gauze, guns. Spilled guts, split lip, slipped disc, slashed tires, surgical mask, stomach pump, siren's song, stigmata. Hair of the dog, *habeas corpus*, head through glass (sweep away blood). Chronic choke. False teeth in Dixie cup, rotten teeth in mouth, face in soup. Roses in room. ("Insurance, please.") Electric shock/electroshock. Epinephrine. Next of kin. Cherry bomb. Air raid. Code Blue, Code Red. None of my wounds are superficial (am I dying for my art?) Tell me: Which is the nurse's button? Which is the nuclear button? Which is the panic button?

Self-Referential

Cin Hochman

I was born on a wild and whipping Wednesday in the wake of ambivalent winds.
I was born listening to the sweet suckling of lambs. I was born with a caul and a calling.

Small as an atom, beating against hard glass, I was born with a shrunken head
and a load of lovely fears, under Virgo and sapphire, in the maternity of modernity.

I was born green with analysis, with pomp and poems, and the ties that blind.
Child of Pushkin and Pasternak; cold as Siberia, hot blood of Ukraine.

I have hovered between illness and ego, pus and shiver. I've been low girl on the
totem pole. I've been something seismic, and cosmic. I've been engorged, entrenched,

enjambed, encumbered. I've scratched your back and you've scratched mine.
I've released my birth certificate and my taxes. I've held my bound feet to the fire.

I have basked in the glow of the glare of the spotlight. I've spit blood through gnashed
teeth. I have licked myself into a frenzy. I've soldiered on, I've melted down.

I have walked with a full heart and bulging discs. I have made love to damaged men.
I've twitched in my fickle and faithless flesh. I've thrashed in my nondescript skin.

I have filed my summons and complaint. I've testified at trial. I've been Exhibit A.
I've settled my case while the jury was out. I've weighed myself on the scales of justice.

I have woken with a wooden spoon in my mouth. I've dug in; I've bowed out. I've
coveted the wine. I've dreamt of diamond ravens beckoning me with their jeweled beaks.

I have walked on rickety sticks. I have seen my lips lose their gloss. I have melted into
water, into waste. I've drowned in moot pools. I've sputtered, gagged, tottered,

and guzzled. I've choked on the bone of madness. I have become the calcified bride. I've made plans and heard God sneer. I've watched my country split its seams. And everywhere I've walked, I've stepped in grief.

Insomnia

Cin Hochman

Facing the allegro moon with a goblet mouth of restless kisses, I am dreaming the breathless dusk with a pillowed head of clocks & daggers, watching the silent guards of black caves tracing midnight's shorn & sheltered face, while ancient tombs of thought screech like chalk across the sandpaper surface on chopped chords of dissonance.

Silk Threads

Claire Ibarra

The front gate is locked,
purple bougainvillea dried and withered–
faded, fragile, thin
      as moth wings.

Fruit trees: ripe chirimoyas, limes,
avocados had dropped to the earth in
abundance. Now the trees are dusty and barren.

When a grandmother dies, a mother dies,
and a small corner of the world is buried–
a world of silk threads
      woven into shawls,
           ponchos, scarves.

Worms in wooden plank beds, feast on
mulberry leaves, weave cocoons, emerge into
dull moths, who lay their eggs and promptly die.

Children live on, marry, have children,
become widowed–leaving a
husband's guitar in the corner
      without strings
         to gather dust.

Recalling music of brighter days,
they will remember the song and dance,
roosters chasing hens, the scent of
cinnamon and roses, the spinning of raw silk
      into thread.

Now the dog lives alone,
behind the locked gate, emaciated
and lonely, longing for his housemother,
who had cared for these living things
    until she became ancient
        –blind, deaf, crippled.

The life cycle of silkworms leaves less tattered
    a garment.

The Rain

RJ Jeffreys

Like a gentle rain
Flows over a coppered cupola
Hazy whispers
Murmur faintly in my ears
I listen to the rain
Through a window
Paned in fog
Behind the glass
Voices distant
Falling down
Falling down
In the spectral hours
Of my dreams
The rain is singing your name
And in your hand a silken scarf
Glides across a spread of scarlet petals
They scatter like raindrops
Drifting absently to the floor
Behind the glass
Voices distant
Still, I listen to the rain
Falling down
Falling down

Down To The Boats

RJ Jeffreys

Down to the boats
The men go
The rough men
The weathered men
The men bent
From the weight
Of the traps and nets
They cast into the sea
And reel in
With a look of hope
For fins and claws
Dipped in gold

A capricious sea is
Where the men sail on
The rough men
The weathered men
The men bent
From the weight
Of the traps and nets
They cast into the sea
And reel in
On anchored legs
The day's fresh catch
Brimming with captured hope

Here I Am at Age Fifteen

Cambria Jones

feeding my grandma from a spoon
and thinking it is pointless. I can't keep her. She's dying.

I myself have not been eating this past year. But that is self-imposed,
and loss is different when it's chosen.

My mother is asking quite seriously,
do I need to leave? She knows death is not a lovely thing.

Neither is life, from what I've seen. I want to hold her fingers
these final moments, leech some of the cancer through her skin.

My grandma barely clouds this cold spoon with her breath. And I am thinking
this is too much for either of us. We've shared everything. Now we're both at a loss.

Her last words come through three squeezes of my hand.
While feeding her, I whispered the same thing in her ear. I. Love. You.

Paean

Cambria Jones

Blackberries ruckling, bleeding crush-dark
bitter-sweet blood—or
                        bygone sword-songs

forgotten.
                Wing-sheen
graying the sky marks geese in flight—or
the dark side of harvest's coming.

Burn the Corn King, fecund effigy
later reborn—or
                one eaten berry's split seed
              becomes second-year's spring green
                      bringing fertile summer,

remembered.

The Landscape of Flight

for Susan and Peter   Lois P. Jones

For once you have tasted flight you will walk the earth with your eyes turned skywards, for there you have been and there you will long to return.
—Leonardo da Vinci

1. Bone

They say a hawk landed in your cradle
and swept its tail feathers past your mouth,
awakening a taste for flight,
your need to pull the buzzard apart

with slender fingers looking for secrets
in the articulated wings. Here
in the late hours the scent of wax burns
your nostrils as you pry the codex,

cracking the contours, drawing
the downy tufts in two. You note
the breast bone shaped like a keel,
lay out each pearled shaft

until it reclaims its shape. Candles
come and go like sylphs, casting shadows
on the freshly inked sketches.
And when you finally walk

the cold corridor to your room, feathers fall
all around you to the tiled floors, lodge
in your velvet robes and pillows.
Sleep arrives
        slender as a wing bone.   You dream you are

a black crane flying low across the Arno,
                the moon a plume nearly gone.

2. Earth

I've been trying for so long
to leave you
I get as far as I can

until gravity pulls me back
maybe my wings are too solid
my breath heavier than salt

bones too dense to lift
into the airstream
too warm-blooded to plunge

into the folds of space
where nothing
answers my call

3. *Flower*

Look at these dogwood blossoms.
Each caught in the act of flying.

Each in pursuit of motion, white wings
bent and touching in a flock

of origami. They could be cranes adrift
in the impermanence of dying. Sometimes

I believe every blossom is another chance
at goodness, the pure silence of a new life,

a hope to be born into it.

In Between Lives

Lois P. Jones

She lets herself be known slowly -
illuminates rooftops in slants of ochre,

bathes the morning beasts, even
as the crow repeats

its darkness. Distinguishes her shadow
by the quality of light. The way yellow

and blue tiles are polished with early hours.
How she angles shade to soften

the courtyard, the hush of the fountain
in a silvered museum. A pigeon pauses

on its bottom tier, falls asleep
in a pool of her warmth. She drifts on

to the next village, lingers over fruit stands
and laundry lines. Mountains return

from where they wandered in the night.
Here is her new mother; chestnut hair

tossed back in a blue ribbon, belly swollen
beneath a linen shift. This will be her

tiny body. She can already smell
the Black Sea.

To the Scarlet Tanager

for Leslie   Lois P. Jones

I don't need a song
to sing for you -

my whole being
is aflame. Bright feathers

burn against the green
leaves, my red breast

where you touched my heart.
This body, blood red

and light. Flying always
gets you closer

to love's source.
My black wings

will tell you that.
It was Rumi who said

we are fire. *If you have doubts…*
bring your hands forth.

The Cobb - Lyme Regis

for Lia　　　　　　　　Lois P. Jones

Always her sea
  coiled like a nautilus
waiting

wound like a whelk
  wintering.
All year she'd saved it

fossiled in her pocket,
  tricked up
in blue.

Barreling down
  from the hilltop cottage
on Silver Street

she reaches shore.
  Now she lets it enter
the way sunlight bends

at an angle. Pulls the tides away
      frees the small bones
at Back Beach,

kneels to the rock pools—
    and what's submerged
fragile as sea eggs.

Weeds weld
     to the Neptune's necklace.
I could live here

she thinks.
     She runs her fingers
through tufts

of pillow weed,
     seeks to know
the periwinkle

and cat's eye snails
    that can live
near the high-tide line.

Her toe turns over
    a large stone
where sponge and sea squirt

survive the dark.
    She takes nothing with her
not even an ammonite.

Lets relics hide
    inside a crevice.
Only a light rain brings her back.

A Ballad for Lucille, Whom I Met on the Shuttle Home

Allison Joseph

Her lousy drunken husband
dropped dead when she was gone,
life drowned in a vodka bottle
when she was out of town.

She loved him through those decades
though he was grossly cruel,
shielding her heart with Al-Anon,
embracing codes and rules.

Now she must plan a funeral
for man who hated her—
who hid the house's deed,
who never sought to cure

his fights with friends and family
his rages and his slights,
She'd wanted to divorce him,
his angry appetites.

The lawyers had the papers
all set for them to sign—
their squabbles over money
had taken so much time.

A widow by default now,
she tells these tales as we
head home from the airport,
laughing bitterly.

She says it's good she was away—
no one could say that she
had killed him out of malice,
had killed him out of glee.

She says she'll plan a time
when family can come
to honor what he was before
he turned to drunken scum.

And then, she'll honor him:
his ashes tossed into the sea,
her life set to begin again—
freed from his tyranny.

The shuttle van drops me off first,
and I wish her all the best.
She tells me she still loved him,
hopes now he's found his rest.

Entreaty

Allison Joseph

Muse, please make me your bitch. I like it rough
and hard, tear-stained and sweat-soaked, inky-fingered
and angry, swollen to brimming with stuff
gone wilding in my head. Anarchy lingers
inside my teeming brain. I need your touch,
your caustic heat that sears and singes,
my body rapt with nothing less than much
more lust than you would ever give. Discontent,
I yearn for you, your never-yielding clutch,
the way you bruise me dizzy, leave me spent.
Yet you stay far away, undressed coquette,
a flash of flesh, unfisted argument.
Each crack of yours that splits my naked back
prepares me for the whip that is your lack.

Accident

Allison Joseph

Catastrophe looms just a blink away.
It only takes an inch to crash and burn.
Just when our luck runs out, it runs astray.

That bone you thought was strong? It cracked today—
and left you limping, unable now to turn.
Catastrophe blooms just a blink away.

The bullet that mowed down a child at play?
A six-year old confined inside an urn.
Just when our luck runs out, it runs astray.

The freighted train spilled into the bay
to make all drinking sick? We never learn.
Catastrophe balloons. We blink away

despite our rules, despite how loud we pray,
despite all debts, raw bruises that we earn.
Just when our luck runs out, it runs astray.

What can we do, in all our rich dismay?
Keep writing, though it makes us itch and churn.
Catastrophe consumes—one blink away.
And when my luck runs out, I run astray.

I did not know

Winnie Khaw

The soul keeps tally of wrongs committed. I did not know. The sun glares at my squinting eyes as I trudge on with my one soleless shoe to look for you. You will not relent. I did not know. Your words are composed in stony cliffs, the winding arcs of seashells, not eddying pools blurring the sand. The blurry luster of dew on my rain-spotted eyelashes do not move you. The soft, loose spiderwebs looping gauzy drapes on my body from the long years of standing, you brush aside. Forgive me, I did not know.

Like glaze on pottery

Winnie Khaw

Me sitting on the porch, you standing at the door.
To wait in patient quiet is not what you do but
here you are. The sunset born in your uncertain gaze
glints off my pupils. I must look through a kaleidoscope
before I can see you. Sparrows flutter just under
dusk, little shadows patter over the ground, sprinkles
of rainfall. Where you are can fit only you … unless
we squeeze. Where I am, there is space enough for us
two. A layer of sheen decorates your face like glaze
On pottery. When you tell me to stand tall, I cower
beneath palm leaves. I have tried to recite the text
but fireflies glitter out from my throat. If two birds
have their wings tied together, neither can fly.

The Painted Forest

Robert S. King

Our stage of Everyman
has no music or balcony scene,
no Rapunzel's rope of hair,
no moral, no Moses
with stage direction tablets,
no swords to clang.
The set is cardboard, a watercolor
woodland scene where trees
huddle together in the rain,
a tombstone leans
from shallow roots,
the cricket crowd is quiet,
and owls don't care to ask.

The line feeder's script,
smeared from tears, dried long ago.
The audience snores but stays.
Wind quietly dies with the fan.
Sound effects have no effect.
One-hand claps fall on deaf ears.

In a three-act play, practice
never makes perfect.
The plot always leads
to the same conclusion
clad in worn-out costume.

No one calls for encore
in fear of the same ending.
Stage right and left the actors walk
off without bowing, forgetting
their parts in the death scene,
knowing that a good tragedy
must end in silence, perhaps
with a songbird dead in the dirt
of an empty forest
and the audience gone home
to their familiar graves.

Stubborn Leaf

Robert S. King

Picture the lone leaf
yet to fall,
the withered face turning
like his brothers
but still holding on
beneath the weight
of ice and explosions
of wind, a leaf out of season
but dancing still
while the tree sags
into winter sleep.

Picture the many births
of reinforcements
he awaits, the new green
leaves taking their turn,
pushing out the old guard.

Picture him as a wing
floating down to the brittle
pile of his brothers,
to vanish in the powder of time

but for the snapshot that saves
him from the fall, that keeps
this lone sentry forever at his post.

The Invisible Man Works the System

Robert S. King

No shadow follows me down a busy sidewalk
where feet of all sizes
and leather of all costs wear down.
Even in chaos the wooden bodies
somehow align along the flow to work.

I go against the flow, bump head-on,
bounce between the lines.
Now that I am invisible, someone else
takes blame for the wrecks.
The nearest visible one is guilty.

Without me, the concrete overpopulates
with the miracle of no one touching.
In order, those seen are those controlled.

Unseen, I infiltrate the obedient rows.
I can be the lane changer or the bowling ball.

The pins do not see me coming.

Letter of Resignation

*after Remedios Varo's
Exploration of the Sources of
the Orinoco River*

Lissa Kiernan

The letter sprouted bastard wings and boomeranged back to me, sealing wax still glossy and soft. Inserting itself in my pocket with a fricative sound, it hissed: *You are not finished yet.*

The river was a cloudy mirror, self-siphoning. A tasseled rope tightened about my waist. All the trees grew petrified but one whose hackles stood up straight. A crystal goblet did a spit-take. The corvids shrilled *tink-tink-tink!*

"But this wine will go to waste," I cry, "and there's a pair of sheepskin slippers I've been meaning to buy, and a cruise I've been longing to take."

"Sorry," the letter stated, "not today. There is a man who wants to see you, there is a man who wants to eat you, there is a man who wants—

So fold yourself twice into perfect thirds and deliver yourself back to him, post-haste. Greet him wearing nothing but your bowler—and try to wipe the weary look off your face."

Dear Leonora,

in memory of Leonora Carrington

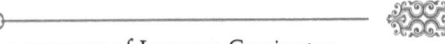

Lissa Kiernan

Why, wily architect, are you not still born? This morning I watched you soar over your *cocina*, hacienda-toned and humming, leaving me to pluck the feathers from my own bloody *tortas*.

Changeling child, answer me this: to stipple the fourth dimension with the third eye, does tapioca tattooed with a squid's black humor work better than a bad clam? I super-collide with Kron, I itch for things concrete: Dirt, masonry, a needlenose plier. Plover, broomgrass, wreckfish.

O Angel of Anarchy, what was your secret recipe? A soupçon of orange blossoms and a pinch of the blues? My late experiments in cookery: I mince hopelessly vague, chop shackled to our collective history. A failed soufflé, one bad thing dispels another. I would be more glad shucking sardines for your flamingos.

But somewhere between thought and gesture oozes the essential oil of our common domesticities. The membrane so fragile now, we dither the sound of green, slurp the scent of river shrimp, burp the sun god's seeds. I hear you passing through me:

Oh, foolish girl, flag your brushes. Stroke with your entire arm. Put more curve in the belly. Use your little finger to balance on. There are only three dimensions: here, now and where the two twine. Beyond the masquerade ball of sex and ragtime, beyond the folly, the dead are partying on the hair of an Andalusian dog.

Fetish

Lissa Kiernan

Love, lay down thy rumpled fur. Let me cut ye
a rasher of bacon. Let me rub ye on the schist

of my skin. On the morrow, ye'll recall naught
but a lingering scent of synamon as thy bow

is plucked in the moldering bloom of another
fool's garden. Look inside, love. Thy moon

wanes gibbous, stars faithless, branches barren.
Time is condensing even as ye part thy lips

to play my bent crumhorn by heart. I am caught
on the hem of your skirt. I hang there—

I am hanging—I am hung. Unworthy to gaze
sideways at thine eyes, dripping thimbles of sloe

fenneled honey, thy lashes cast down, mad luna
moth's wings. Can ye not see I've gone half-wolf-

mad? Consumed by what is foregone? My cucumber
beetle, my pigeon pie, my short-nosed sturgeon?

I promise three times to be discreet and vow
profusely this is not about money. Speak to me,

now. Am I enobler or enabler? I wish only to lick
the soles of thine feet with gentle flicks of my mother-

less tongue. My God, do you walk on these things?
They would make my kingdom come.

Mermaid - On Hanuman

Usha Kishore

He happened upon me, like
the storm, untamed elemental
ballad, enemy god, monkey man,
primeval force, rugged and lusty.

I, Suvannamacha, golden mermaid
fervently wooed by a fearsome foe,
who set golden Lanka on fire
with a sweep of his flaming tail.

His limbs bore the fire of stars,
as he shape-shifted like light
upon the sea, until darkness engulfed
us both in a whirlpool of rising tide.

His hair redolent as marjoram,
wind flung on some rocky ledge,
as his hands slipped from the top
of my diademed head to the tip

of my golden tail. His fabled antics
lulled; impassioned, he courted me
on whirling waves and in sea caves,
shell latticed and framed with pearl.

I am concubine to a strange creature,
who wraps me in myth; his love as lucent
as the sun the sea swallows each day.
No pain, no guilt to taint this bliss.

I tasted his lips until I, winsome maid
of the sea was made of air; my hands
stole the power of the tempest
that raged in his rippling muscles.

In his primate eyes, I read continents
waiting to be conquered; his dreams
anchoring us between the sea
and the sky, the surf dancing

his desire. Under a monsoon moon,
with sea gulls screaming treason,
I drowned my Raksha deities
in swirling eddies of passion.

I watched the lights of Lanka fade, I heard
the mourn song of the sea, as he sailed
on my tail, murmuring sweet nothings
that ached like conch whispers.

My father's life grew cold, while
my heart grew warm in his love;
his chaste monkey fate rewritten
in an epic that roamed the seas.

As we parted, he left a seed with me,
my trial of fire, his conquest guile.
On windswept seas, I wait for him,
bearing my sorrows in a pot of gold.

Raksha or *Rakshasa* - demon

This poem is inspired by the Thai myth of Hanuman and the Mermaid Suvannamaccha and the famous mural painting in Wat Phra Kaew, Bangkok. The story of Hanuman and Suvannamaccha is a popular one from Ramakien, the South East Asian versions of the Indian epic, Ramayan. During his conquest of Lanka, Hanuman, the monkey god falls in love with Suvannamacha, the mermaid daughter of Lanka's demon king Ravana.

The Mortician

Laurie Kolp

I never thought I'd meet him here,
the man who just a year ago
was homeless. I never thought
I'd hear the scruffy wraith
zonked out on a park bench

speak of mortal options
cremation, burial—
which is more complex,

choosing the right coffin
for a conked-out carcass
sure to resurrect a zombie,
leaving mourners with an empty shell
sharply clothed, caked-on make-up
masquerading what appears a mannequin,
then entombing to a dwelling hole;

or incinerating bones to dust,
sprinkling ashes over one of seven
wonders of the world in whirls of twilight
zones where apparitions wander free.

I say it sounds as if he's biased, that he'd
rather burn than bury.

He asks if I'm a gravedigger,
I bite my tongue and say I'm not—
I much prefer warming by a fire
in winter's chilling hell.

Tree of My Heart

Victoria Korth

Oh specimen, Hevea brasiliensis,
I'm stuck on your numbers
and must offer you something
to take them away, the height
your grandfather stood, master
of the canopy, not uneaten canapé
guests quietly crumble into your soil.
I need to describe you, adjective
you, but hold back, dear neutral
presence. You bring me carnations
and small change when I am ill
or on my way to church, kind
cousin to fungi, root making stone,
wall-eyed fish I will never lay eyes
on, you (have you) seen them along
your cell lines, your thwartedness,
your earth also my shoe, grow me
out of this mineral pot, this heart.

Lessons

W.F. Lantry

Our first step is to see: open your eyes
as we descend the rose and thornvine slope,
weaving between the shadows. Afternoon
fills fertile woods with writhing summer heat:
the copperheads are out. Broken limbs, strewn
by lightning, block our way, and one vinerope
hangs from a branch where our clear path begins.

The second is to know: look for the fins
of tiny fish beneath the log-bridge shade,
watch how they turn in unison. Along
the curving bank, note where the deer retreat
at our approach, and how hidden birdsong
seems background melody when antlers fade
between bent maples as the warbler sings.

The third is understanding why the wings
of herons open as our steps draw near
their fishing ground, and how their graceful flight
remakes shadow and song, how blue wings beat
in time with other rhythms: flashing light
and shade remaking every song we hear:
echoes transforming as the great wings rise.

San Dieguito River

W.F. Lantry

The sulfur wings of butterflies ascend
these paths more easily than I can climb
the bouldered face of this dry waterfall.
At times the river travels underground
or flows beneath the stones, unseen by all
who search, unknowing. Look for stands of thyme
or wild rose if you would find a spring

along these slopes. No mockingbird will sing
to guide my steps, always towards the east,
careful of scorpions and rattlesnakes.
I've seen their marks between the stones and found
their cast off skin. Here, where the laurel shakes
beneath each sudden wind gust, and the least
small breath of air disturbs the sawtooth grass,

I know the nightly coyotes' footsteps pass
across this path I travel. I have heard
their voices calling from a moonlit ridge,
as if their lamentations could surround
whole valleys with their darkness. From a bridge
I watch the water's glass reflect a bird
in flight, a heron, with his blue wings spread

across the same wind, passing overhead
and moving toward the sound of a cascade
further upstream. It promises some rest,
at least a place to linger, and its sound
will drown those pressing voices. Near the crest
of this long ridge, at last their sound will fade
where even songs of birds and crickets end.

The Curse

Rustin Larson

Each time I try to write a few lines,
Someone demands my attention.
Today, someone wanted Shakespeare
In large type. I'm not complaining.
It's a good thing.
Right now, the window is bright,
And you'd think the world was deserted.
I pause to listen to the sound air makes.
It does have a sound, you know.
A very delicate fabric being torn, endlessly.

Bumble

Rustin Larson

Perhaps this is precedent, perhaps not,
But when I was a kid, a bumble-bee
Flew down my shirt. I stood trembling,
Calling my mother's name, hoping
She'd hear me over the washing machine
And come rescue me. I made
A decision then to quietly slip out
Of my skin and become unreal,
But I was not fast enough.
The creature gave me a sting
Which lasted for years.

The Artist

Rustin Larson

Self portrait of the artist playing an ivory ukulele
While riding on the back
Of a Bengal tiger. Lemon-lime leaves
And tangerine flowers
Are marzipan confections.
There is a dark chocolate lion
Peeping from the ferns.
All you can hear
Is the roar of the orange tiger
And the plunk of the ukulele.
The artist is smiling at his cleverness.
The lion is silent and stern.

Increasingly Speaking of Rain

Ann Neuser Lederer

Doves hoo, evoking apnea.
Ear trains to await.
An old man forms a triangle:
thumbs and fingers frame new sun.
Still waters run deep, pointed accusingly.
A face sees a mirror at the bottom of a well.

Through mist unnaturally warm
for this time of morning, something like mercury
but red, expands, spreads, turns, and becomes.
Here is the day, it announces.
The forms of rituals soothe.
A boy is already lifting into the air far away,
unseen, there, attached like a thread to helium.

Saint-Rémy de Provence

Stephen Linsteadt

A whale of rock jumps out of the land
and freezes above the earth;
the backdrop to "Starry Night"
painted close to where green bathed
the artist's vision in a yellow
        tainted room.

The scent of Languedoc
still warm about your neck.

Thunder uncoils over the night.

Rain on my umbrella
drops of deep mystery. Madness in May
only warm iris blossoms understand.

Their light whispers
and won't hold still.

You can't complain I'm singing
        this is an asylum.

And where are the human beings
who once lived in the olive groves?

We were compelled to keep our distance
        from the chapel.

Pigeons cooed then waited
for the echo to reverberate
off its stained glass walls.

Crossing the Yangtze

Dennis Maloney

We cross the Yangtze
on the new concrete bridge
into tomorrow.
Last year we would have
crossed on a ferry.

The river, wider
and more immense
than my imagination allowed.

The river of countless poems
of poets going in or out of exile,
or sailing off to a new post.

But today hulking grey barges
carry the iron ore and steel
from the belching factories
of the new China
out to sea and the world,
the sky a dirty hazy of grey.

We cross the Yangtze
on the new concrete bridge
into the future where the
road you are told to follow
is smooth and the only thing
worse than having choices
is being unable to choose.

Finished Business

Alexandra Martin

Say the dead walk
into the next field, find

their anger heavy,
ledgers dragging

at their ankles. Say they uncurl
the memories of fists, release—

not phantom limbs but phantom
pains, all that remains on this

side of things. All they
have lost, all that it cost

to escape the war.
Say they do return

(thinking—what—
of the urn?)

to stall at the camellia
in its crown of leaves,

to flex old muscles
of dis-ease. Would they dwell

with us
now that they're undone?

Would they not go quickly
back, to un-become?

Blank Verse

Alexandra Martin

There is a time for
internal rhyme but
it is not now, not
on these greased and crumb

strewn chairs, puke green
of the ER waiting room
at Hollywood Presbyterian.
On some white cot I can't see,
blood drips from my love's
thigh, from the gash where
The mugger jabbed. Rust
blunt blood lust.
Kay Ryan, I have no
patience for your beauty
right now, no stomach
for anything but greasy
chair despair, for the light
that unbidden
slips in.

Blue

Matt McGee

The commencement
echoes across the street
like a day 18 years ago
when she said "I went
to the store and bought
one of those little tests today."
The daughter he would have named
Katie might've been marching out there today
if the spinning marble he lived on
had been just a little
more blue.

Bach's Little Anna Magdalena Book

—Prelude in C Major Ken Meisel

"I will write for you the music of your orgasms,"
he whispered to her as they gazed up into

the plum-colored night sky to watch the stars.
"I will do this for you, you whose name means

sinner at the gate with the voice of a meadowlark…"
Keeping his delicate fingers arched over the keys

so as to be free to pass his thumbs beneath them
as he caressed in quick, sexual motion each key

of the harpsichord, each quill rising to pluck
the string above it, like gently striking at the edge

of her small ear lobes so as to awaken the
meadowlarks she'd hear inside herself when

they made love, the composer moved steadfast
to write each note. This, as he did penance

for engaging in and playing unseemly variations
on the organ in a church, and this because he'd

served time in jail for an unruly dismissal, and this
because the angel Azrafil had visited Bach

one evening as the composer strolled alone
down cobblestone streets into a cayenne sunset,

each cloud a celery-colored hue, each building
toasted in a daffodil flambé, each new fugue

piling up like voices in conversation with each other,
like competing sea gulls jeering in the wind or

like a contraction of women singing in roulade
beneath the arborvitae in delirium tremens

as they awaited the resurrection of their souls
to the gray watcher who stood lonesome at the lake,

and the angel had told Bach that he'd lose his eyes
because he was using the tips of each finger to see, –

"and I will write for you these notes," he said again
to her, "until my fingers become red as strawberries

and until my eyes ignite – listening to you as you
raise each voice above the pedal point in you, while you
come."

My Wife & I

Ken Meisel

My wife is a rhythmic meridian
        I am allowed to cross.
                She is fixed there on the bow string
of the fiddle of beauty. She is the fiddle string of beauty
        as all girls are once they break off
                the axis mundi tree
where girls are rhythmic loops of expression
        and then emotional violas
                with lipstick and tits that fool us.
Lips are beauty accessories
        on the meridian lines of mystery.
                Boys don't know how to fly kites
in the meridian lines.
        Punching each other as sublimation doesn't help
                doesn't graze beauty well.
                      Nor do the horses they ride
against the feminine sky –
        which is the meridian line I cross
                when I am the broken
physics of desire
        trying to kiss
                my wife.

Los Angeles Eyes

B.Z. Niditch

You speak of angels
here with an unrolled tongue
up the ladders and angles
of success
as I meditate
in the lotus position
from my transition
of bedtime stories
hoping my sailor suited ways
and boyish ways
on the open stage doors
will embrace me
like everyone else
on Hollywood and Vine
but arriving here
as a kid with one rust suitcase
everything is not what
appears behind the ears
and courtesy is a card shark
and a publicity agent
wants only his own
and a panhandler is hungry
and there is always
Loves Anonymous
where ex rose bowl queens
sell their crowns
in pawnshops
and a cool piano player
may be a musicologist
and motorcycle jackets
will not go out of style
and light weights

will play the heavy
and a Beat Poet
survives
the youngest of mornings.

Satan's Antlers

Richard King Perkins II

Satan is always busy in hell with his well-defined routine
but he'd rather be sipping lemonade and primping his hair
on Catalina Island.

Satan only rents hell, and that, somewhat reluctantly.
He spends most days trying to figure out how to rise from
the abyss of the world and levitate back to his place of birth.

His singed wings will only fly him a few feet off the ground,
so he remains malcontent, misanthropic, jealous of humanity—
its eyes wide with the promise of salvation and the caressing
of souls.

Cruelty is most deceptive. The growths from his accursed head
are most often mistaken for horns. But the doomed will tell you,
that Satan's antlers are unnatural protuberances, calcified knots,
great lumps grown from the repeated knocking of his skull
against the uppermost barrier of Hell.

Even Satan seeks respite from damnation, trying to flap a body's
length closer to all he has forsaken. His last and only hope—
to again soar through the pure clouds of heaven, performing
superhuman aerobatics, all for the pleasure and approval of God.

Tom O'Bedlam in the Garden of Eden

Anne Elezabeth Pluto

I get pulled back so easily
your voice, your eyes, your need
and I reappear, open and happy
to the next day that suffers me to stifle
the sorrow - the beautiful early
autumn weather - perfect
I am in it alone - the silent
house where you never see me - don't ask
I won't tell but open myself
to your body frightened and charmed to an Eden you
were taught, but don't believe last night we
watched the Tigris and Euphrates flow, vulnerable
I will myself not to deception but mercy to forgiveness
and your love which unsettles me like the weather
a tempest fit for Tom o Bedlam himself - naked and
disguised - leading the blind and the crowned
into the light.

The Roseate Scarf

Brie Quartin

It's the one you bought
from the milliner just west
of the train station even though
it was August. We had paused
at the storefront to remove sand
from my shoes, a vanilla Coke
and a knish still in hand from the guy
who sold lunch out of a shopping
bag to the strollers and fishermen
on Sheepshead Bay. You threaded
the wool under my hair, wrapped it once
around my nape, drew me in like a cigarette
and exhaled my name upon the wind.

I came across the scarf again a week
or so before you left. It had weathered
sixty summers and countless stares
from others who thought it odd attire
for the time of year. And on your final
day at home I wheeled you down
the length of our sidewalk, seared
my name into your mind burnt black,
and wrapped you lovingly into its soft,
exquisite fringe.

dark days

Cindy Rinne

my body cheek
fur motionless on frigid
steel black-
tipped tail hear me
out I dream of drinking
melted snow locking
antlers shed velvet
innards carved out
how did it happen
new scorpio moon
rising fireplace
crackles in camouflage
clothing you
prepare to cut
my skin

mapping

After "Eyes As Big As Plates"
by Hjorth & Ikonen

Cindy Rinne

you weave a helmet
of branches from
fire they orbit
your head like
medusa or map lines
wild grasses
masses of neurons speak
to the pads
of your feet crushing
reike symbols
cancer vines your
lungs mapped lungs
respite rasping exhale
light on galilean moons
births another kind of human

Fragments

Mary Kay Rummel

Violet-haired Sappho
praised purple hyacinths
crushed beneath the sandaled feet
of passing soldiers.
Praised amethyst
last color before dark.

Praised women who lie down
in wild thyme, purple crocus,
who wind sprigs into unbound hair,
who speak dill and quince-apple
shaking pollen into shapely ears.

Ancients said the head of Orpheus
washed up with bladder verach
on her island, still singing.

They called her tenth muse,
genius deformed by gender.
Called her harlot, burned
her poems.

She escaped the flames
in fragments we translate,
ashes we rearrange.
Thousand-petaled, she is sifting
down to us.

The Road

Mary Kay Rummel

Time thick in your throat on the road to the land of the dead.
—Theo Dorgan

Way before Giza where she lay
in a sarcophagus, the pharaohs
being compact creatures like herself.

Before she left the chant and trembling
in Malta's Hypogeum,
womb deep inside the earth.

Long before Glastonbury,
she signaled boats from the Tor.
Before Malin Head, another ship's graveyard
crashed around her.
Before there was a lighthouse
on Inish Trahull, earth's oldest naked stone.

Even before she lived in the abbey in Paris,
her eyes filled with the wraiths
of women who came to wooden gates
carrying sick bodies of their children.

Way before the windowless house
on the Mississippi, or the convent walls
she knew were unnatural for a girl with wings.

She took a wrong turn somewhere,
but that was before she followed
cracks in stone where the light inside
breaks through into meadowsweet and gorse,
all thorns, no leaves, golden blooms.

Reading Zagajewski in Prague

Mary Kay Rummel

At a black marble table in the Cafe Louvre
your poems pull me deep into hallways
worn with age and graffiti where the city
wears black undergarments and eternity
dresses in ruins.

Poland is your home, near enough
to feel your spirit in these cobbled streets
still peopled by men in black wool,
caps pulled low on their foreheads.

I could find you on the corner where a string quartet
plays Mozart, melodies threading the screams
of generations, in the bass and treble clef
of Dvorak's Cello Concerto, or at the Jewish memorial—
names carved into the wall, names like bird song
in the saddest neighborhoods.

Your poems flicker in eyes of gargoyles,
wander among rooftop saints
where classical and rococo hold hands.

I could find you in the square where parents, professors,
clear-throated flutists and poets await your greeting,
the dead and the living threading plazas,
church yards, like deep fish through dark rivers.

Soon I'll sit on a bench facing the sea.
While Prague's blooming trees still quiver,
I'll remember the gold and cream of the city
and your words, moving in its shadows,
branches of kelp inside the waves' green swell.

Mare tentaculorum

Peter L. Scacco

Emaciated light
barely endures
the abbreviated day
until no tone is left,
the pale day dissolving
before the mind discerns.

Engulfed in the chill air
all the plants lie numb
in terra-cotta pots,
the Charioteer wheeling
through night's encroachment
toward apogee.

A deep solitude
splays its vast tentacles
through a sea of darkness
overcoming all who cling
to faded day, not knowing
the stars that dream above.

Syllabus

Rebecca Seiferle

Years ago, I dreamt of the only teacher I loved.
I dreamt that one evening I ran into her at a lecture hall,

she was coming out, her mouth still full of words,
a sheaf of paper as usual in her hands,

and with her was a small girl who began skipping and running
around the edge of the room, as

we stopped to talk in that old impossible language,
I began to watch the child, noting

her dark hair, those cropped bangs.
She resembled me at the age of five. A friend at the time,

fond of psychology, when I told her the dream, said
that child must have been my true self,

but I would hate to think that we are brought back
finally to nothing but ourselves.

In the dream, she seemed to belong to me and my teacher,
as if it were true that some loves

give birth to spiritual children. But she seemed more
than some imagining of winged lightning in the air.

When she stood between us, my teacher introduced her
saying, "her name was Japanese for firefly."

I understood then that was the end of all the *materia*,
the *alma mater*, between my teacher and myself

that struggled into words, pale larvae eating
their way through the damp decompositions of papers;

leaves like papers, the forest littering the floor,
rose up in that one moment's

fitful incandescence, as if all the riddles of love and being
had been concluded in a name.

And still I do not know what it was . . .

Love has no children of its own

Rebecca Seiferle

I thought it was the thought of you thinking
as you watched the fireflies falling

into the undefined, endless, fields of night,
only to light up again, in the very depths

of the damp grass, thinking that their lighting up
was like many small anxieties lifting within you

that reminded me of the presence of fireflies
in this world. I don't know why they were never gods

or God's messengers, but perhaps all recognition
is no more than memory, the words subsiding

like hatch and larvae back into the earth. The way
my heart does, for years at a time, struggling through

a long darkness of materiality, heavy as the soil
it must burrow through before unexpectedly

entering another season of light, though,
when burrowing with a mouth full of mud, my eyes

clogged with roots, the earth is never a way
or a road. There's no expectation of release

and the suffering has no meaning. Oh, I tell you,
I could lay at your door, all the wreck and ruin

of the heart, the ancient attitudes of love,
all fear and cramped grasp, and ancestral whining.

But all I want is to stay awake, to see clearly
in the dark or light, to stammer my way

through the hedges of words, toward that presence
that seems to be *you*,

clear as a firefly
on a darkened plain, but vague

as anything that has retained its own mystery.

she thinks of her hands

Rebecca Seiferle

last night she was contemplating

the one chunk of cedar left over
from last winter's burning

trying to see in its grain,
the shape of her hand upon your thigh;

she was thinking

she could carve
something for you,

but it would have
to be

the curve of your breast
in the red veins of the forest,

small enough to be placed on your altar
of precious things,

or, perhaps, her own heart carved into a necklace at the feet
of your Buddha, where that tiny spider

of a wish that longs to weave itself into existence
disappeared just the other night,

and then she started thinking
she could take

that bookmaking class
on the weekend, learn how to

make pages of paper,
aromatic, light green, *yours*,

full of sea mist and fog, salted with the taste of her own
book that you could write upon as your fingers

write upon her shoulder...
giddy and giddier, she takes the pen from me;

writing this, she
laughs and looks at me as if I were an dear idiot:

don't I know
it is the fever she feels for you?
the fever

she feels
in her hands...

whatever it is, it's the power
that gives her back

the power
of her own hands.

Being Born at Any Hour

Rebecca Seiferle

I don't know why there's fog, the desert as if
pregnant with some vanished or impending sea, or why
waking up, I'm wondering into it, remembering those lines
by Auden "many have died for lack of water, not one
has died for lack of love," except that it's my birthday
in two days, and his poem was written a year or two before
the emotional climate into which I was born: sad decades
where everyone would die for nothing *but* the lack
of love, stillborn, held in insensate arms. Still,
just as the limberbush sputters back to flower at the touch
of rain, something rises, sings, on the blue lips of the infant
who, in us, is always tunneling toward the light. I don't know
why at the stillborn level of misery (the way my head just yesterday
crucified its third eye), something touches down and springs
back up. It's like being reborn at any hour, the earth's
generosity in my body and in the morning air.

If the animals within you are quiet,

Rebecca Seiferle

you can listen until the half moon sinks
in the dark vapor of a cloud whose rain
will not fall and hear only the domestic
snuffling of your neighbor's two small dogs
at the one splintered opening in the fence
or the squawl of a cat in heat in the alley, and,
if you stay up long enough until the sun begins
to lift the false dawn of a bluing sky,
the distant crowing of someone's rooster.
The first time I heard the roar of the lions
I was looking through the shimmering leaves
of the one grapefruit tree that roots in the yard
at my Kuan Yin statue, her black body of mercy
riddling the leaves with presence
and absence, as the tips of her fingers and the hem
of her robe were beginning to flake off
and crumble, meditating with the sun and the moon
and the clouds and the tree. Startled out of the miserable din
of the animals within me, I did not know
they were lions; their voices so abrupt
coming over the fence transported
the sun and the moon into the lost savannahs
of their skins, veldt gutturals not knowing what voice
spoke to me, what was it I heard. Real lions, not like
those who style themselves as lions because
they stomp their little feet and gnaw at every
corner of their kingdoms, but the creature itself,
and in time, in their roaring, I began to hear
the truth that remained free in them even
as their teeth broke on the concrete edges

of insurmountable walls, and then the other
animals came to me, one by one, the muted
trumpetry of the elephants who seemed to know
their voices did not have to swell to carry across
the circumference of their kenneling, the egrets
and seagulls with their awkward sea cries
arcing over the yard as the monsoon rains created
new ponds and streams to fly to, the cacophony
of a troop of monkeys, erupting like a chorus
swelling for human recognition, and the cry
of some animal that I still do not know. And
sometimes at night, nothing but silence. Silence
breathing wider than the sky from those living
bodies kept in a zoo for viewing like
the miniature ceramic horse I was meant to be—
there, up on a shelf and wearing its label "Work Horse by Enesco."
How I needed to divorce myself from that kingdom,
though I did not know what awaited me or how I needed
to hear the living voice of living lions, all the creatures crying out from
each tiny ark of the covenant, calling us home
to ourselves.

Dusk Going Home

LeRoy N. Sorenson

On some slow evenings, sunlight hangs in the air
disappearing in small slices as the patient night
opens its mouth.

These evenings feel like going home, those hot humid
days in mid-summer, men mopping their faces with a slow
practiced motion, sweat seeping between young breasts;
the grass sticky underneath old elms and fresh mown lawn
permeating the heavy air. Streets lined with Victorian three
stories and Queen Ann wraparounds. Gray-haired women
sipping cool tea, slowly rocking, ice cubes melting in tall
glasses. Delivery trucks clogging commercial avenues, denim
shirts sweat streaked as drivers unload beer cases and black
bourbon. Dark bars, musky blues and quick
damnation on the juke boxes.

And the city's backbone—a churning Mississippi—barges
moving as through mud, boat captains resigned to another
thousand-mile trek. In the east, above sagging trees, a sliver
August moon and faint stars dripping, the darkening,
overarching sky magnificent as a lover, head bowed,
slow breaths, sweet sweat.

The Armstrong Boys

LeRoy N. Sorenson

The last time I saw the Armstrong twins
together, they were staggering down Main, arm in arm,
their eyes blinded in a setting sun. How they

reeled, unbalanced, how unwell they were—
laughing at some private joke only drunks share,

their big feet tangled with the coming night.
How they went to Nam to swelter, to dive
into holes, dirt and foliage littering their thin

shoulders. How they waded knee-deep
in paddies, leather boots rotting on their feet.

Haze of napalm, orange dust.

Then, there was the day they entered the village. Silent
except for barking dogs; the headless bodies,
the squad kneeling in a center clearing. And a howl

when they saw the children skewered
on bayonets, tongues bloated black. How removing
a small body blew one brother's legs off, left him

holding in his entrails and how, much later,
the remaining brother returned to bar stools.

Double shots before him.

Among the Survivors

LeRoy N. Sorenson

My hometown reeked with its meat
plants and cattle yards. As a child,
I rode my red Schwinn, standing
on the pedals, from the shanties
on the north end to small town excess
on the south. I rode with a baseball cap
pulled low over my face, down
to the river bluff and the stench
of sour blood; then the graveyard
nestled against river bank and on
to the abandoned plant five blocks
west of the dingy motel and bar.

All this I remember, but have forgotten
when I first saw the photographs—
solo and group shots of men
and women standing in dust yards,
coats wrapped tight like shrouds.
Houses with no paint and dogs
with heads slumped to the ground.
I remember a picture of my grandfather
flirting with his daughter-in-law—the raw
energy in his body, charm transforming
his face—while she grinned, eyes lowered.
Another of my sister squatted next to a bare
garden. Grandmothers thick with dead
children and births. And my favorite
sorrow, counting off the missing faces:
both grandfathers, my favorite uncle,
my brother. My mother, buried
in herself so far; and my father, lost
into every imagined life but his own.

And I remember how, once, on a chair
in the living room, I listened as my mother
moaned, the air so thick with a grief
I could swallow; how I kissed my first girl
near the meat plant—her mouth
injury and danger. As we caressed, my eyes
stayed open, and I looked across empty fields,
the crushing loneliness of fall twilight;
and I knew this girl, like all
the coming others, had no idea
how deep my haunting ran.

Running With Wolves

Ron Starbuck

Let us run with the wolves of desire and memory.
Where we are not that far removed from the wildness

that still clings to us in dreams unfolding, before
mirrors white with winter. Across worlds where

ancestors inhabit our bodies with breath and
spirit, who breathe together through

a veiled gate that marks an entrance to eternity.
Nothing is lost here, nothing we do not already

know in the bright bones of our memories.
We remember well, the taste of Eden, which is

wilder still than our imaginations may even
now envision. Let the oldest wisdom lead

us onward with eyes open wide in wonder,
under a midnight of stars, tracing infinite light

streams of the spirit. Let us bow to the wolves'
bright passing across constellations

of thought and consciousness,
unhurried from one dawn to the next.

Wizard & Whiteface Clown (*Zen Priest*)

Ron Starbuck

In tribute to George Jisho Robertson, a wise old soul and friend, an Anam Cara.

the old wizard
sits with a winsome smile
a knowing look

the visage of a wise
whitefaced clown
bears its marks

with laugh lines
and wrinkles
well earned

he lights one more
cigarette, not his last
by any means

a reminiscence perhaps
of an ancient amulet
a shaman's talisman

the smoke drifts upwards
curls around his head
as visions and dreams

if you look closely, you
may see Buddha sitting
under the Sala tree

a Naga Prince sheltered
by a king cobra
in safety from thought

forms without number
with a piercing vision
he looks up

his students bow
politely, sit in promise
and smile back

nothing is said
between them
there is no need

there is only
this moment, here now
complete now

it happens subtly
letters and symbols
begin forming

wordlessly they speak
and then something
breaks through

beyond thought
and form
silent verses

poetic language spoken
between souls, in a single
silent tongue

in that silence, in
this infinite openness
they rest as one

one world arises and passes
away, then another
and another

mirrored in
thought, in breath
where all

creation moves
in wordless expectation
in stillness

to be still and
fully known
as mystery

"When I was a child, I spoke like a child, I thought like a child, I reasoned like a child; when I became an adult, I put an end to childish ways. For now we see in a mirror, dimly, but then we will see face to face. Now I know only in part; then I will know fully, even as I have been fully known."
— *1 Corinthians 13: Verse 11-12 (NRSV)*

Roget's Thesaurus

Donna Baier Stein

In the beginning, the word.
Language particularizing
(detailing, itemizing, describing) nothingness,
revealing the rich flurry of everything.

I loved this book as a child. I love it now.
Somehow I knew, even then, that
this is where it (life, I) could be found.

For how would I speak to you without words?
How would you know if I loved you?

I don't want to do a found poem here,
listing word after word and straining
for connection between them.

But there's all that life between the covers!
From microbes (germ, minute thing, organism)
to perspective (outlook, distance, view).

Do you understand what I'm really saying?
That there's a space between nothingness
and the namings, a space where you know
even before you learn what any word means.

Meditating...

...on the oval leaves of the azalea bush,
their edges curling into a cup,
a prayer, ready to receive.

...on the tufted titmouse skittering on branches,
looking for all the world as though all the world
is a leafy, verdant playground.

...on the wind chime dropping from the rafter,
its five thin copper fingers
shimmering in the wind's whisper.

Beyond, the field expands.
A hill slopes, dry leaves and fallen branches
form a coat of one color, brown, in variations.

I could go on: the flat stones laid as a low wall,
the moss green bird feeder, a tower of well-seasoned wood,
tulip poplars and red oak rising to sky.

All this just within the frame of my window!

And outside the frame, books on shelves, rows of photographs—
signatures, cities, dates. A leather chair. A slice of lemon floating
in water.

And even further, through a different sense,
I see my dog on the couch in the room behind me,
his heart curling in sleep, a prayer.

Before Counting the Cost He Follows Her to the End of the Road

For Michael Formanek   Robert Strickland

It's all steel-toed and bricks down there,
nickel-sized love.

Dimes through holey pockets
clinking down the dotted universe

black and bridged over,
chain-linked message clear, the fear

of one-way solitude.
Her head bobbing like a magic marker

fuzzy at the tip, carelessly used,
too many stringy edges

in the border dust,
drying out, uncapped.

He clacks over cobbles
bopping through no particular key signature,

held in check by carefully dropped triads
and the guardrails of groove.

Around the curve it all stops
sudden, brakes jammed to floorboard,

carpet worn through by leather heels,
down into love's cul-de-sac,

all for the rub
and spare change.

Passage

Robert Strickland

She was there that morning,
the coffee and cinnamon air
moving carefully up and around
obstacles left on the staircase
in haste. Those mornings stretched
to years, from apartments to houses,
from pediatricians to tuition, overlaid
on a changing geography, growing
like the time that passed quickly
down streets, around corners,
ever running away.

She is there this morning, hair
still soft around awakening eyes
adjusting to this Colorado sunrise,
her taste for coffee strong
after thirty six years, a simple waiting
that leads slowly into the day.

We sit among basil, begonia, and blue daze,
the cat crouched for the unsuspecting crow,
the owl retreating at first light,
severed hindquarters of a rabbit
left under the Russian sage
by the satisfied coyote.

We Are the Universe

Melissa Studdard

Watching your mouth as you eat I think
perhaps an apple is the universe and your body
is an orchard full of trees. I've seen the way your leaves
cling to the ground in fall, and I noted then
that your voice sounded soft, like feathered, drifting things
coming finally to rest. Note:
I was the core in your pink flesh. You
were hungry birds
and foxes walking though the miles of me.
You climbed, dug your nails in my bark, yanked
something loose. Don't tell me what it is.
Just keep it close.
Because I planted these rows
and rows of myself for you—
so I could lick the juice from your lips,
so I could remember
how round and hot
the promise of seed. If I could find
that orchard right now, I'd run all through the rows
of you. I'd stand in the center and twirl
until I got dizzy and fell. I'd climb high and shake
until the only thing left in you was longing,
and you'd write a poem for me. You'd say:
Your mouth is the universe. Your desire
is an orchard full of trees.

Oran

Tim Suermondt

> *from a terrace a woman's*
> *voice cries ooh!*
>   —Italo Calvino

Even in the distance,
while I try to rub the palm leaves
and the long night out of my eyes,
I can see she's beautiful,
delicately poised in her white robe.
Her ooh! sounds sweet as the sea air,
the sea that takes a few more grains
from the foundation of the Grand Hotel
and sends them all over the world.
I stagger a little through the square
but keep what little dignity I have intact,
heading in her direction, both my hands
for effect and thanksgiving on my heart.

Keeping Up

Tim Suermondt

"It looks like the trees bloomed overnight,"
my wife says, and she's right.
Even the train tracks and the elevated highway
in the near distance have a spiff and shine
I never noticed before.

Not that there is—but if despair were present
it would momentarily be obliterated.
The thought is enough to keep me going,
reminding me that much is still
possible no matter the skewered odds.

My brisk steps as I head to the grocery store
will surely give me away.

The Circumference Of The World

Tim Suermondt

A humming bird, a thimble,
a runway bigger than many towns.
Slacks hung in the closet, panties
draped over the sink, a museum
of antique cars, a bowl of chocolates.
The milk tree, the endless dilapidated
cul-de-sacs, the mornings announced
by the bored rooster, nights by
the crickets brash as opera singers.

Consolation

Maria Terrone

To weave a blanket of words
pulled tight or loosely looped—
tough words built like sentries
that stand against pain
in its quiet calculations,
then its sudden rush forward.
Or words that shout O!
over and over, hoops big enough
for happiness to leap through,
tail raised.

A blanket to pull up
and tuck below your chin
at the end of the day
when speech must pause,
or to cover your face
when night stalkers hover
so they can read every word.

The Animal In My Purse

Maria Terrone

tugs, makes a groaning sound deep
in its throat.

It could be a hunger-growl,
Buy a loaf of bread on the way home,
or a message from the front—
how the war is going, distant news of famine.

There is no knowing, as I know
nothing of the next hours marching
off into my future in a disappearing line.

When I stare at the sea, I divine nothing
but a mute, mirrored wall.

Still, I fear the peril of willed ignorance.
So I grope, grasp and place my lips
to the heaving animal's black heart.

Solitude

Charles Thielman

She dons a robe of silence
leaving the burn-pile of love.

Reviewing her life-spread maps,
embers spiraling down, she notes

the junctures, the choices, hears again
the crack of bets flung at reality's walls.

Well past being tripped up looking back,
she knows how solitude vases the rose stems

of unspoken needs. Pushing face first
into sandpaper wind, her dream

of flying brought down to wishbones
snapped short. Her gaze reaches inside

the forest's quivers of moon-light.

A Painting, An Early Morning Walk, and All the People

Charles Thielman

Faces of this age, inbound,
transit under city towers.

    Tip of paintbrush inside canvas rivers.

My eyes wander in a white sky,
drawn as human
to our magnetic stutter,
hands in pockets.

    Distant jackhammers cube the air.

Trees wanting a wet gray shine,
the strokes of a sable brush
lay cart tracks down on
canvas gravel, through pools of water
reflecting November overcast
and the skies of a seagull's cry.

    Let the vandals worship their statues.

At the bus-stop,
I stand back and watch
children make churches with their hands.

Feather

Angela Narciso Torres

The almost-neon sheen of moss
spreading like a stain on
the ash tree's grooved bark,

the hammock's frayed rope
to which goldfinches return
each June, needling, trailing silk

to their nests, but mostly the quiet
of a neighbor's house, white
drapes billowing, bring back

those summer silences
I moved in as a child, a shadow
slinking through empty rooms.

Dust motes tunneled light above
the cold floor where, belly-down
I sprawled, goose feather in hand.

If I lay there long enough,
if I brushed the feather
on a fixed spot on the pebble-

washed floor, how long before
I'd make a dent? The point
is not that when night fell

there was barely a scratch. The point
is how, armed with a feather,
I believed I could make a mark.

Garden, End Of Summer

Angela Narciso Torres

Black-eyed Susan, coneflower, China rose—
all that remains when I return, blooming
without irony in my spent garden.

When I left my mother it was July
in Manila, the strongest monsoon in years.
Thirty villages buried in mud.

How could I know, two months later,
that she'd awaken in a white room
in a white gown, her plastic wristband

a reminder of her name? My mother's
eyes appear as from the deep—
one minute glazed, the next,

burning holes through a window,
listening for footfall. Who is this
woman without her nocturnes,

painted saints crowding her nightstand,
the mute phone winking day and night?
Whose face, unframed by kohl

and rouge, no crimson lips
pouting at the mirror
to bear her into the day?

I deadhead the roses, carry them
to water. The flagstone
empurpled with petals.

August Moon

Angela Narciso Torres

The summer before his second
brother leaves for college
our youngest makes his bed

on the landing beneath the skylight
where the stairs hinge.
Soon the family will shrink

from five to three,
two sons away, one
at home. How will it be

to breathe the thinned air?
To move within walls emptied
of shadows that shimmered

with their banter, sweat,
and heft? Past midnight
I find his crescent shape

plugging the stairwell,
a blue slip of moon
in darkness, breathing

Stay
don't go
nobody leave

The Scarab's Tracks

for my niece Katherine Jon Tribble

In Maadi, sunrise shifts heat
across ragged palms, bending

their rigid poses like divers
arching back in perfect

falling motion. Behind the jigsaw
four-foot stone wall, Katherine

spills cool water over impatient
poppies, cleansing dusty petals

bright as sirens, bright as her
fine hair seared white-gold molten

by morning's arrival. She coaxes
fat red wasps down about her,

untwirling a sweet bun like
an African river wrinkling its way

past crocodiles and staunch
secretary birds, twisting and

lapping into dark alluvial fans
unfolding rich deltas, feathers,

graveyard bones of banyan and
lost ivory. Katherine pinches

back anthills at her sandaled
feet, traces a beetle's tracks

with her big toes furrowing
the sand right up to the shiny

carapace glistening over its
ball of earth. Inside, her mother

soaks tomatoes in a warm sudsy
sink. She'll peel them later

and she and Katherine will turn
the sweet pulp on their tongues,

taste late summer in the flesh
and seeds of the luxuriant fruit.

Acero

Kenneth Weene

On the morning of his last corrida
Manolete did not pray to the virgin.
What need for divine intervention?
From the vantage point of eternity,
Cervantes, leading the swaybacked Quixote,
laughs at such a hero's conceit.
Little boys with swords and capes, they
believe the legends of El Cid; they
drive the moors from Vietnam and climb
the mountaintop of Iraq, these kings,
who pissed the campfires of childhood
as if true manhood lies between the legs,
as if the truth of thigh and groin could
bleach the color from the crimson sand.

Mountain Lake, September

Helen Wickes

An old chair by the lake keeps rocking,
maybe a ghost has come back for the view.

Sadness fans out, the where have we been
all this time, as piece by piece,
we're nibbled back by the greedy air.

On the sand six people wrestle on masks
and wet suits, their rented second skins.

I'd like to rent a second skin,
one to put on and peel off at will.

All day the El Dorado forest on fire,
and the smoke, sucked over the mountains,
circles South Lake, probably late

for a rendezvous with a blackjack queen
up in Reno. I can't see through the smoke.

Can't think through the wet-suiters' laughter,
wish they'd shut up.
Which they do. Gone into the cold water,

they leave behind a palpable vacuum,
the world much bigger than we thought.

In the water six dark heads bob in a circle,
and that renegade smoke sneaks over the ridge,
heads home to the burning, home to the source.

Summer's Drift

Helen Wickes

On a man's wrist, on a horse's breath,
the dead find purchase and beg
to be taken along to the mountains.

For grace we cultivate an extra layer of dumbness
and say yes to them.

Many people stay lucky,
often wanting too little. Not so the fire.
It pounces from one tree's crown to the next.

In childhood the melancholia is incurable—
a constant let me see you. Despite beauty
and years of kindness, the fracturing continues.

I should take my soul to the river twice a year
and wash the meanness out.

Poor words, they were never the danger—
Illumination, it's a physical thing.

From way up here the river, the traffic
are all one sound. Let me watch the fan lift and set down
the hair on your neck. Lavish hair.
Now look—red and yellow with a smattering
of black and white—boy birds accessorize so well.

Imagine not being alive to this, I say,
to this—after 12 years our tanager returns.
Well, maybe he's not the same tanager.

For The Hour

Pui Ying Wong

Let there be coffee, eggs
enough for two,
sun to escort the gulls
and students off
to field trips, buttons
on their cardigans
gleaming,

clouds to leave en masse
like tiny islands
liberated from earth,

dragonflies to tilt
their wings, showing off
their unique heliograph,

poplars to fill out like girls
in prom dresses, mysterious
and still growing,

Deliver me from the marsh
of sleep, hissing
dreams of cockroaches
and rubber-tongue lizards, let
my love greet me
at the table, his arms
sprung open like windows.

The Weight Of Air

Pui Ying Wong

The streets in this town hug
the neighborhood in a curl.
Brownstones tout their heavy past,
stained glass, candelabra,
gas lamps glow in a swirl of dust.
Morning washes the flagstones white.
Black birds flit to and fro,
shadow into light, light into shadow.
Memories untangled from time's thicket.
I've exhausted even speech, even speech.
Might every poem be a prayer,
a horse's neigh upon a precipice?
I've wedded to this earth, to its fruits
to its perils, I've held on
like an air root, like an air root.

In Summer's Evening

Pui Ying Wong

Friends gather in a jasmine-
scented garden, drink
wine from Sonoma and listen
to tales of travel: Tuscany,
Chartres, an ashram in India.

Then someone says the President
is a war criminal, and no one
contradicts. The talk turns
to the number of dead, the cost,
whom the war serves. At last,

sounds of leaves rustling take over,
we say goodbye, returning
home, returning to the wars
which lurk in ourselves
    in insomnia,
    in the purge hours.

Features & Interviews

Melissa Studddard
Radio Host with Spirit and Poetry to Share

by Mark McKay

There are as many motivations for writing poetry as there are poets; some of us write to entertain and amuse, others to educate and enrich, many write exclusively for themselves - for the catharsis of getting feelings down on paper. Melissa Studddard writes to communicate a profound sense of wonder, joy and awareness, to express a deep compassion for all living things. She is adept at multiple literary disciplines: poetry, short stories, novels, fantasy, young adult, middle grade, children's, spiritual, metaphysical, interviews, and creativity journals.

Melissa Studddard's spirituality is not based in any one narrow tradition, mythology, religion or creed; she borrows from many and sees the good in all. Her essence is inclusivity - we are all invited to share in her vision.

Born in Alabama and raised in Houston, Texas, Melissa gained her B.A. and M.A. from the University of Houston and later an MFA from Sarah Lawrence College in Yonkers, New York. She is a professor at Lone Star College, Houston and a teaching artist with the Rooster Moans Poetry Cooperative.

Studddard is very active in the literary community and on social media forums, and keeps her worldwide fan base informed via her website at www.melissastuddard.com.

Our younger readers in particular may be familiar with Melissa's novel of spiritual journey and enlightenment, *Six Weeks to Yehidah* (All Things That Matter, 2011), for which she garnered both Forward National Literature and Pinnacle Book Achievement Awards. This unique book and its accompanying journal *My Yehidah* are used in schools across the US to introduce middle grade students to spirituality.

Others may know Melissa Studdard as the renowned host of Tiferet Talk, the online radio show which has featured many poetic and spiritual luminaries such as Charles Simic, Robert Pinsky, Natalie Goldberg and Ed Hirsch. The uninitiated can catch up with the fascinating on-demand episodes by visiting www.blogtalkradio.com. She has also transcribed several of her most inspiring interviews in the recently released paperback *The Tiferet Talk Interviews*. Besides her work as a talk show host, she is a professor, a book reviewer at-large for *The National Poetry Review*, a contributing editor for *Tiferet Journal*, and a teaching artist for *The Rooster Moans Poetry Cooperative*.

Studdard is one of those writers renowned for fiction who share a deep and abiding love for the most condensed form of creative writing. Her poetry is replete with the same sense of spiritual wonder, sensuality and vivid imagination which characterizes all of her work. Her eagerly anticipated debut collection *I Ate the Cosmos for Breakfast* is available now from Saint Julian Press.

Poetry

It seems appropriate to start with this short homage to spiritual teacher, Ram Dass, which encapsulates a lot of what Melissa Studdard stands for; lovingawareness, mindfulness and open-hearted acceptance of our place in the great scheme of things. Sample some of the magical tapestries Studdard can weave with words:

You Are the Tree of Life
—inspired by Ram Dass

>Say to yourself, I am lovingawareness,
>and feel all the birds of the world
>come land on the branches of your heart.
>The cage of your ribs was never meant
>to trap things in or keep things out
>but was always only there for love
>to land on. Be aware that in your branches
>lies a nest, and in that nest lies a batch
>of eggs—fragile, delicate, and new—
>that it rests with you to incubate all
>that you will hatch, over and over
>through the endless birthing season
>of your life. You are the world
>to a million small creatures
>you may never even have noticed.
>Everything you do matters. Be brave
>in this life. Say it to yourself—
>I am lovingawareness.
>And let your heart be a home
>for all the cherished things
>you know must fly away

Melissa has the rare ability to be spiritually instructive without being didactic or preachy. Her poetry reflects her deep humility and understanding of how, in spite of our insignificance cosmically, we can all achieve wondrous things through the power of love.

The last line does what a great last line should, leaving us in a deeply contemplative state; pondering the impermanence of all things, the fleeting nature of our own existence, the need to cherish those fragile butterflies of love, contentment, wonder, innocence and spiritual enlightenment.

Our second offering is quite different and demonstrates Melissa's mastery of ekphrasis. Here she unpeels the layers of meaning in a Remedios Varo masterpiece.

Sudden Encounters
—inspired by the Remedios Varo painting Exploration of the Source of the Orinoco River

> The Orinoco overflows from a goblet,
> spouts from the center as though
> water had wings. I'm telling you,
> this goblet rests on a table
> in the hollow of a tree—so
> deliberate that you can't help
> but question if the almighty
> watchmaker set it there himself.
> Paley would have had his say,
> to be sure, but this is about Varo
> and her own fantastical teleology,
> about how the source is never
> what you would expect, how
> inspiration swims like pink dolphins
> through the rivers of night, daring
> you to look into its eyes, challenging
> you to brave a lifetime of nightmares
> for the purchase of a moment of genius,
> to be like the woman manning a vessel
> no one else has ever seen, like Varo
> herself—swimming on the river
> with wings, her retinas burnt and open
> by frequent, sudden encounters
> with dark and unholy gods.

The source of poetic inspiration or muse as we often describe it is indeed mysterious and often hard to navigate towards, though Melissa seems to have tapped into a rich vein with these poems. It should perhaps be pointed out that they were written at different stages of her writing career, over a number of years, and therefore represent a journey of discovery. Even for the most talented inspiration is seldom if ever a faucet which can be turned on at will. These poems are as hard-wrought as they are finely crafted.

In "Killing The Moth" Melissa is again inspired by a painter, but surprisingly on this occasion by his words rather than his brush strokes. Is the life of a moth worth the sacrificing to be immortalized in oil on canvas? The moth in question is the subject of Emperor Moth, 1889 by Vincent Van Gogh. Van Gogh's words are tinged with regret and compassion, and the poem probes this dichotomy before ending on a simply stunning metaphor.

Killing the Moth
Yesterday I drew a very big, rather rare night moth, called the death's head, its colouring of amazing distinction ... I had to kill it to paint it, and it was a pity, the beastie was so beautiful.

—*Vincent Van Gogh*

> The flapping of night-wings by a fire,
> a rattling in the skull,
> a moth, its wings cloudy white,
> tinged carmine and faded green:
> all is captured in a sigh of pity—
> beauty must hold still to be seen.
>
> And what is death to the dead
> when art gives wing to the living,
> when what was gauzy and frail
> presses its form to imagination's
> human shores, there to be held,
> foam swept through quick passing days,
> there to withstand the turning of seasons?

The leaves will be green again,
brown again, gold, and green again.
The leaves will be red.
Red, and the death's head moth still flutters,
steadfast, swept beyond the joy and danger
of a shift in wind.

Artist, have you learned the moth?
You are more alike than you can see.
Not in the way a night can swarm to flame,
but like a gust of stars
breathless with foretelling—

the markings, like the lines
that streak your palm, tell of leaves
pressed into a book. Their color fades.
They rot. They leave behind
an imprint on the page.

Next we find Melissa pondering the timeless legend of Icarus through the medium of John Sokol's fantastic painting Icarus Practicing. What price the impetuosity of youth? But then again, how many feet-on-the-ground years equate to one moment of heavenly flight?

You Were a Bird, You Are the Sea

—inspired by the John Sokol painting Icarus Practicing

Stretch them wide
as God's first breath.

From tip to tip
there is no time.

Just the rumbling
of a tune

in your makeshift
beak, and bright

sky galloping
through the hollow

of bone. Bucket
of air, spine built

from light, boy
full of flutters

and drafts—you
speak mountain

stream, laurel leaf,
rolling cloud—

the dialect of flight.
The world drifts

like a madness
inside you—earth,

trees, and birds,
feathers, wings,

and night, the start
and end of time

rowing through
blood's currents,

sailing inside
the freedom

of mind,
now split open

by a whirlwind
of koan, pushed

like air through
sky's vast lung.

 When I go,
let me go

like you, Icarus,
past my own

limits before
I fall. Let me

be a flesh-toned
streak in the sky,

a flash in the blue,
a sunburst

of wonder
rejoining

the ripples
of sea.

Our last offering for now is a most tender, heart-rending little love poem which displays Melissa's mastery of imagery, metaphor and simile. As with all of her poetry and prose, this poem is spiritual in the broad sense of being engaging for the soul as well as the intellect.

Eminent scholars have debated for millennia as to where the soul resides, whether in the blood pump in the "cage of our ribs", in that most mysterious and fragile organ, the brain, or even external to the human body. One thing is for sure, Melissa Studdard's soul shines like an aura around her and she manages to transfer this somehow to the written page, a rare talent indeed.

A Prayer

> Someday I'll meet you again,
> and we'll sleep like the eyes of hurricanes,
> lidless in our trek to taste each other's tongues
> as they throw dirt over my face and into the quivers
> of my throat. I've been meaning to say a little
> something each night, to light a candle
> in the doorframe, set fire
> to the empty church: For you, I'd drive

the people back into each other's arms,
where they could see, finally, your
softness again. I meant to say I knew you
were unhoused, the original nomad. There were
none living there among the pews. What was left
was pressed among the pages of psalmody.
And this is no new thing. Another costume off:
My golden hair. My blue-green eyes. Shed beneath the dirt.
I meant to say, how are you? And, also, this is not about
me. Because there are tigers scratching
at the swirling wind. And there are monsters
banging on the shutter doors. Because I've had
no time to think or eat properly or rest. It was all
just a blind sneeze in the wind. Let me know everything
about you, please. I'll go back. Do it right this time.
I'll be a dragonfly, a pebble, an earthworm, a flea.

We would encourage readers of all ages to seek out *Six Weeks to Yehidah*, which is an intriguing and rewarding short read, available both In print and digital form.

Please drop by www.tiferetjournal.com which is a fantastically broad church of literary talent and spirituality, and also www.blogtalkradio.com/tiferetjournal to catch up on the inspirational interviews – we can't think of a more enriching way to spend forty minutes.

Personally, I can hardly wait to get my hands on a copy of *I Ate the Cosmos for Breakfast,* and hope Melissa can find time in her hectic schedule for many more volumes in the coming years.

In Conversation with
Poet and Author Melissa Studdard

Interviewed by Mark McKay

Many of our readers will be familiar with your very popular novel *Six Weeks to Yehidah* **and the companion book** *My Yehidah*. **Where did this extraordinary tale spring from and how did the project come to fruition?**

> For several years before I wrote *Six Weeks to Yehidah* I'd been devouring texts— philosophy, comparative religion, metaphysics, spirituality, wisdom traditions, and more—all non-fiction. I kept thinking how great it would be for kids to have access to some of those ideas. But I was also acutely aware that kids do not want out-of-school reading that feels academic or informative. The desire to share those ideas in a non-academic way was the fuse that led to *Yehidah*.
>
> The match that lit that fuse was a prompt I got in a writing group. We were asked to read The Oxford Book of Modern Fairy Tales and write our own short tale. As I worked on the prompt, I realized that the whimsical narrative I was creating would serve as an ideal allegory for some of the concepts I'd wanted to share with children. I was so compelled by the zany characters and their symbolic value that I kept writing and writing until I realized I was no longer working on a short story. I was drafting a novel.

Tell us a little about the Tiferet online community and Melissa Studdard's part therein. Your interviews with eminent writers on *Tiferet Talk* **are fascinating! Let's indulge in a little fantasy for a moment. If you could interview any three writers, from any genre and any era, who might they be?**

> Tiferet is the brainchild of publisher Donna Baier Stein. The name comes from the sixth sefira in the kabbalistic Tree of Life, which symbolizes the reconciliation of opposites, such as compassion and strength, and intellect and emotion. The focus of the community is to promote peace in the individual and in the world through creativity,

tolerance, and connection. It's about seeking common ground as a place to nurture compassion. The online community hosts blog posts, writing forums, workshops, and all sorts of other wonderful features. As well, Tiferet supports a magazine, a publishing house, and the radio program. Regarding being able to pick any three writers to interview, I've already interviewed such spectacular people that I could say my wishes have been fulfilled.

But, to answer your question, let me choose from among the impossible—those no longer with us. I could name hundreds. Oh, don't make me pick! Here are the first three that popped into my mind: Julian of Norwich, Walt Whitman, Sojourner Truth.

You make no secret that spirituality plays an important part in your life and writing. In these days of technology and the instant gratification culture, as organized religions seem to be struggling for relevance, what part do you see spirituality playing? Might you consider yourself an evangelist of spirituality?

This is a difficult question on so many levels. Thanks for challenging me. First, I'm not an evangelist. I'm just a humble writer. I don't see my views as any more important than anyone else's, and I don't preach; I share. I wish everyone wrote and shared their best ideas.

How much we could all learn from each other!

Regarding the current role of spirituality, I see that it suffers the same indignities and enjoys the same perks as so many other things in this instant gratification culture. That is to say, it has become wider and more shallow. Most of us more frequently encounter spiritual material now than we did just a decade ago—there are spiritual quotes and uplifting stories and photos all over the internet, but the fragmentary nature of these encounters does not lend itself to the sort of deep and prolonged reflection that allows us to integrate important teachings. So, the good news is the frequent exposure. The bad news is the lack of context. I hope people are making up for that lack of context in their offline lives. I hope if someone sees a quote they love by Thich Nhat Hanh, they go and buy one of his books or download a dharma talk. I hope when people are moved by a prayer or a great passage from a holy text, they take the time to memorize it and really reflect on it. I hope when people are excited by a news story about a charitable organization, they donate time or money. To be nourished spiritually, we must do more than graze.

A little bird told us that you are nearing completion of your first full collection of poetry *I Ate the Cosmos for Breakfast*. What a fantastic title! How have you found the process of putting the book together? When and where can our readers get their hands on a copy?

Thank you for asking! It will be available early fall in hardback. The digital version should follow shortly after, and then I believe the paperback will be out about a year later. It will be available through Amazon and Barnes & Noble, and through many fine independent bookstores and libraries, as well.

I'm so glad you like the title. Putting the book together has been, by turns, delightful and agonizing. Trying to organize the poems feels a bit like attempting to get a group of unruly children on a playground to stand in a straight line. As soon as you think you have order, one of them pops out of line and has to be coaxed back in. But, how enchanting it is to work with those unruly children!

We had our spies out in force at the recent AWP conference in Seattle and someone fitting your description was spotted. For those of us who missed out this year – give us a wee taster of what it was like both in the venue itself and at the satellite events.

AWP was fabulous this year. There were so many events going on simultaneously that sometimes I had to attend half of one and half of another. Some offsite highlights for me were the Pirene's Fountain reading, the Tiferet reading, and the VIDA ball. At the venue, I thoroughly enjoyed the panels I attended, as well as the book fair and signings. I learned about many, many new authors and came home with a bag full of books. But the best part was meeting friends I'd previously only been able to interact with online or on the phone. Everyone was better in person. Every single one of them.

Thanks for the great questions, Mark. It was a delight to be able to speak with you.

Jon Charles Tribble
Academician with an Editor's Eye

by Lark Vernon Timmons

Jon Tribble is a man on campus making a big impact in the literary field. As a founding (and now) managing editor of the well-respected *Crab Orchard Review*, and series editor of the Crab Orchard Series in Poetry published by the SIU Press, he has edited over 50 poetry collections and manuscripts to date.

Like many fine writers, his pen-to-paper interest initially grew out of an early appreciation for reading and books. He recalls writing verse (of a sort) through the primary and middle grades and by high school, had added journal editing to his skill set.

> *"I've always found the process of discovering a poem through the words I bring together one of the most challenging and satisfying experiences I can imagine."*

Born in Little Rock, Arkansas, Tribble grew up in a church-based camp devoted to medical and social services programming called Aldersgate, located at the time just outside of his place of birth.

He's called a handful of states "home" and his background and experiences, particularly in the workaday world, are varied and many—as dishwasher, maintenance worker, fry cook, movie theater manager, data processing clerk, and security guard.

My parents crossed
state lines, not oceans; leaving
the red clay of Alabama for Iowa,

Nebraska, Arkansas. Our journeys
might go short or long; it doesn't
matter. Beyond us, in the open

water, two pilot whales breach and
blow spouts of sparkling mist into
the sunlight. Their dark backs

break the waves before diving, and
we know as we imagine maps
and routes they wander, wherever

they head toward is home. As
we stand against this constant
wind, we still know the way.

Excerpt, **Blue Crabs**
© 2010 - 2014 *Prime Number Magazine* - All Rights Reserved.

Tribble received his B.A. in English from the University of Arkansas at Little Rock, and an M.A. and M.F.A. from Indiana University at Bloomington, where he worked on the staff of the Indiana Review on and off for five years, including a year as editor.

On perusing and choosing others' poetry for publication, Jon says:

"Most of all, I look for poems that make me want to keep reading, make me feel rewarded for the time and attention I give them, and make me want to take them to other people and say to them 'stop whatever you are doing right now and read this.'"

He is the recipient of a 2003 Artist Fellowship Award in Poetry from the Illinois Arts Council and his work was selected as the 2001 winner of the Campbell Corner Poetry Prize from Sarah Lawrence College. His poems have appeared in numerous journals and anthologies both in print and online.

Jon resides in Illinois with his wife, highly-acclaimed poet, Allison Joseph. He teaches literature and writing and directs undergraduate and graduate students in internships and independent study in editing and literary publishing for the Department of English at Southern Illinois University, Carbondale.

IROQUOIS BRAVE

Experiencing Jon Tribble's poetry is to discover verse born out of fascination, curiosity, sensitivity and honesty as in this excerpt from the beautifully-titled coming-of-age poem, "Whisper Trees:"

> What I can't remember is the color
> of her blouse, though I know the way
> the sun lit her blond hair as he
> brushed it free with his fingers,
> the blue barrettes she always wore
> joining the growing pile of their
> clothes. I was eleven, always
> following her to the lake where she
> worked summers as a lifeguard, and
> when I saw them go into the woods
> I trailed behind, stalking them like
> an Iroquois brave from the *Leather-
> stocking Tales*, avoiding the dry twigs
> better than Natty Bumppo ever did.

Excerpt, **Whisper Trees**
Contemporary American Voices A Journal of Poetry, April 2012

Day After Night After Day

"Poetry about work has always fascinated me as a reader, whether the work is recognized in the larger cultural and historical ways...or the poems explore the intimate ways work can shape our relationships with others or our environment or our sense of self."

Inspired by his own experiences in the fast food industry, Tribble has written a series of poetry with the purpose of sharing "day after night after day of the work itself"—which gives the reader insight into the price one pays for the things we as consumers have come to expect as cheap and easily available at drive-thrus in cities and towns all over the world. Two previously unpublished selections from this interesting project follow.

Lightning Bird

> Every night at closing, the brick red tile
> floor flooded, a swamp of soap and steam
>
> and bleach, so each kitchen outlet reached
> down from our fluorescent heaven of
> the stark godless ceiling with 120 volts
>
> of possibility and problem. So many heavy
> cords snaking up like black vines climbing
> the greasy air to their rapt connections,
> male/female bond reproducing alternating
> push and pull of stainless steel electric
>
> tables shimmying their sifting snow banks
> of clumping flour before the glue of egg,
>
> milk powder, and water left only papier-
> mâché strips of random skin and bloating
> fat behind. Spinning its ocean web of salt-
>
> water into the ever-thirsty flesh of the bird,
> the marinator tried to tumble away on its

own wild ride, the boxy motor on shaky
wheels carrying the out-of-tune steel drum
full of bumping birds from walk-in to kitchen

and back, so we knotted tight one dry towel
after another, securing the unruly plug

to its home in the outlet above until some-
body forgot and I reached up to grab
a damp clean conductor demanding my

sudden cymbal crash of shock and stun
to floor—an avalanche of weighted power

crushing my inner light beneath the world's
singe and spark and flash of deafening heat.
When my ears could see again, my eyes

heard the polyester angels descending
with bright faces of forever now trying

to reshape a clay familiar with something
finding shudder, hesitate, pause, playback
and start again, caught between fiendish

commands to cast me down to the damp
pit yawning underneath me and seraphic

insinuations to raise me up to their pillows
of humid spice, welcome my shattered mind
back to their clouds of diminished light.

How Not to Get Robbed on the Night Shift at Kentucky Fried

> Someone has more than chicken on the mind these summer nights.
> Lock the doors. Not at ten-o-one or -two. Close the lobby
> but don't pull down the shades till three—you want the cars to see
> you mopping in your red-and-white striped shirt. But don't forget
> someone has more than chicken on the mind these summer nights.
> Check the peephole three times at least before you turn the bolt
> and drag the heavy trash across the lot to the dumpster
> close to the walk-in Taco Bell that gets held up each week.
> Knock four times then two then four again to get back inside.
> Someone has more than chicken on the mind these summer nights.

W*aiting* F*or* N*ighttime*

Here, in one of his poems reflecting a long time interest in fishing, Jon shares the experience of night fishing at Devil's Kitchen Lake, a man-made lake created by the Civilian Conservation Corps in the 1930's:

Midnight Rainbows From Devil's Kitchen

> The lantern dims and sputters the little light
> we need to wait in the dark for the lines
> to pull, release, pull, and—taut at last—
>
> set the hook and play the catch around
> the other four lines waiting, their purpose
> to weigh the night in against our careful
>
> measurements and patience. A constellation
> of baitfish scatter like some new universe's
> primordial moment, the crappie and shad
>
> bumping the nearest poles slink into green
> shadows beyond us, and now the headlight
> floating in its foam ring illuminates the flash

and run of this twenty inches of muscle
straining against its life's breath burning
up the blood. We'll net and ice the fish

soon, cut the length and spill out what's in
back to dark shelf of oxygen layered cold
below us in the table of the lake, but now

the splash and dash, the leap of color
our eyes can only hope to prism holds
us here until the limit, and brings us back.

© 2010 - 2014 *Prime Number Magazine* - All Rights Reserved.

Particularly satisfying about Tribble's poetry is that not only are we drawn into his experience, we are also drawn (back) into our own. As I acquainted myself with his writing, I consistently felt literally or figuratively, as though I'd been "asked along for the ride." I believe there is no finer example in this regard than his narrative poem, "Up and Down Wye Mountain," which is so simple and profound in its beauty that on the first read I heard myself utter a reverent "Amen" at poem's end.

Up and Down Wye Mountain

    Daffodils crowning the summit
    of the country church-topped hill
    have begun to pale and wither

    from the sun and heat of Arkansas
    summer, though the earlier
    hymn of flowers' open mouths

    brought out the city dwellers
    to the festival the congregation
    here celebrates every year.

But it is the church itself which
calls us, our pilgrimage
a journey to familiarize my mother

with this site and one other
the Bishop appointed her to lead.
Her recent vocation has been

rehearsed with sermons, ceremonies,
and assisting in the rituals
that embody the articles of faith,

reaching beyond response
which a lifetime of supplication
has taught to lead the call,

but, at sixty-eight, she now seeks
to test the strength of her
calling anew, to discover if this

challenge is the path study
and long prayer mean to bring her to.
My father, my wife, and I

have joined today, all of us, perhaps,
a bit skeptical and concerned,
but also warmed by the enthusiasm

apparent in my mother's
sharp attention to all the practical
concerns: how long it takes

to drive from home, gas stations
or of their lack upon the way,
the safe and unsafe speeds to wend

this winding trail.
My wife steps out first and then
the rest of us stretch

and gaze about at this calming
scene, the handiwork
of masons resting under the oaks.

The stone church appears
to be locked tight, but a back door
guarded only by a blue-

bellied lizard opens and we enter.
There is much more here
than any of us had dared hope for:

kitchen, Sunday school
meeting room, an organ and piano,
and the simple solid altar

and cushioned pews the sanctuary
presents us with exceed
every expectation and demonstrate

the care of belief and duty
we might or might not find evident
in storied sacristies

housing relics of less humble
design. Attendance
figures from the Sunday before

show "38" adults on hand,
"15" children, and a collection
of "$143.85" with "$20"

added for building and grounds.
My father wants a picture,
and though my mother refuses to

pose for him, my wife
and I take turns standing behind
the sturdy Communion rail.

We head down the hill to Bigelow,
six miles away by road
—though the hawks we see rising

in the bright sky might
make the distance less than three—,
and my mother wonders aloud

why two small congregations are not
one, though she says she
would not rush either church toward

a change neither might want.
As we reach the bottom of Wye Mountain,
the rich flood plain for

the Arkansas River slopes through
stands of pine and tangles
of honeysuckle on Toadsuck Ferry

where the now lock-and-dam
tamed waters are traversed much more
easily, though perhaps less

often since busy interstates have
cut off these back roads.
Bigelow approaches with promise

at first, a horse farm
shadowed back amidst the loblolly,
a cattle ranch with heavy

Bhraman hybrids sinking in a stock
pond's cool mud. But as
we near the single railroad track

which marks this town as
here—along with its beige aluminum-
sided post office—houses

begin to seem to sway as much from
poor construction and
disrepair as from the humid heat.

Our first attempt to find
the church finds us turning around
at the mobile home assembly

yard that must be this town's only
industry, though scattered
insulation and a cemetery of unused

metal frames appear to be
permanent monuments to prosperity
long past. A second try

leads us back and forth dead-end
one-way streets, but there
are few enough that by process

of elimination we end up
in front of what a weathered sign
tells us is the "United

Methodist Church," though easily
we could have mistaken
the style of the scrawl painted

here for a "For Sale By
Owner" posting. With no apparent
parking site and the ditches

flanking the road choking with tall
weeds, I ease the car
onto the crossover leading up to

the white wooden building
which teeters on its cinderblock
foundation. The squat

steeple points toward heaven only
indirectly, seemingly
concerned in this world with

the thin shade in sight
some hundred yards away. My wife
and father get out, but

I remain with my mother, who now
gasps a bit from the close
air. She fans herself and tells

how this church has lost
members to death and relocation
the last decade, how fewer

than two dozen names appear on
the current roll—maybe
fifteen or twelve active members:

Not a growing ministry.
The job here would be staying
the decline, and perhaps,

attracting a new congregation,
though from where it is—
at best—unclear. When my wife

and father returns with
the word that the building is
locked, their survey

of the exterior is grim indeed:
rotting doors stacked
carelessly against the outside

of the church, mildew
and what unstained paint there is
flaking and peeling off

—an erratic layer of dandruff
spotting the surrounding
ground—, no visible electric lines,

—though a rusted-out
window unit belied the absence
of power—, and stairs,

front and back, warped and loose
and waiting for any
misstep to send someone tumbling.

"Someone should burn
it to the ground," my father says,
despite forty-five years

working for and with the Methodist
Church. "If you've got
a match, I'll do it right now."

But my mother is calm.
She says this challenge is what
she prayed for. We all

wonder how this forgotten church
has kept its charter,
but slowly my mother's resolve

takes hold of us doubters
until my father even begins saying
he will transfer membership

to this church, work with them
to clean and shore up
the damage. We drive back past

the chapel atop the hill
on our way home, understanding
a little more the devotion,

the need to serve which shapes
my mother's calling.
A week later, the Bishop joins

my parents for their
introduction to the congregation
of ten at Bigelow and

the members of the church welcome
my mother and father.
Then the Bishop tells the church

how happy he is to find
them supportive of this newly
licensed minister on her

first appointment, and suddenly
the recognition strikes
them, they want to know what

the Bishop thinks he is
trying to pull on them, that surely
he doesn't expect them

to receive sacraments from a woman.
Recounting this later,
my mother says, "It was as if I

were no longer there
the moment they realized I was,"
and her voice is weary,

even as she goes on to describe
her surprise at the beauty
of the sanctuary: six tapestries

resplendent on the walls
following the Gospel of Christ's
nativity, His ministry,

the Last Supper, Gethsemane,
the Trial before Pilate,
and Calvary's hill. New hymnals

rested beside dog-eared
Bibles in the plush red-velveted
pews. She said they had

polished the brass to impress their
new pastor, decorating
the heavy oak altar with yellow lilies

bowing beneath the dark
shining wood of the empty cross
suspended from the rafters.

c. *storySouth* (Issue 36: Fall 2013)

Many thanks to Jon Tribble for his time, talent, poetry and kind permissions.

Recent Poetry Credits

In print:

"Hooking Up" and "Surrogates." Prime Mincer Literary Journal 1.1 (Spring 2011): 130-133.

"Long Stories about Short Pigs," "Compared to What," and "Up for the Down Stroke." South Dakota Review 49.3 (Fall 2011): 69-78.

"White Christmas, Blue Velvet." South Dakota Review 50th Anniversary Issue (Fall/ Winter/ Spring 2012 & 2013): 205-210.

Online:

"Spirit Currency," "Conversations with the Dead," and "Tangle of Shadows." A Poetry Congeries at Connotation Press: An Online Artifact (Issue 11; June 2013).

"Risen" and "In the Hall of the Mountain King." The Account: A Journal of Poetry, Prose, and Thought (Fall 2013).

"Air Strike." The Enchanting Verses Literary Review XIX (November 2013): 16.

Also visit Crab Orchard Review and SIU Press

In Conversation with Professor and Poet Jon Tribble

Interviewed by Lark Vernon Timmons

Jon—So good of you to take time to share with our readers... What were your earliest experiences reading and writing poetry and how did they influence your formal education and career?

The earliest experiences I can remember reading and writing poetry are very separate from one another. Growing up, I was a big reader of mythology and, other than the King James Version of the Bible, I probably spent my first serious time reading poetry in verse translations of Homer and Virgil. I especially enjoyed reading and re-reading The Odyssey.

Writing poetry was a very different matter. My first attempts at any verse I remember were when each year the Little Rock City Beautiful Commission held a slogan contest for the Little Rock Public Schools. The first time I entered I did very well (probably third grade); the second time (in fourth grade) I entered I was disqualified for writing a slogan that was too close to something by Thoreau, even though we hadn't read any Thoreau in my grade-level (though, to be honest, I usually read my sister's readings and she was in seventh grade) and I certainly had no idea at the time what plagiarism was—I was barely writing cursive; and the last time (fifth grade) I entered I also sold slogans to other students on the bus with me—I placed, but one of my other slogans placed higher—and though my teacher suspected me of selling my slogans, I had learned my lesson the year before and everyone I did business with never admitted it.

Also, in eighth grade, I wrote a series of Civil War poems about Gettysburg, Shiloh, Andersonville, and some others I no longer remember and would be very embarrassed to read again if I found them.

I'm not sure any of this shaped my formal education and career path. I really believed I would be a computer programmer when I graduated high school. And I spent nearly eight years managing movie theaters, which I am now writing about.

The *Crab Orchard Review* is in its 18th year—that's excellent! How long after you joined the faculty of SIU Carbondale was the *COR* founded?

I began working at Southern Illinois University Carbondale as a lecturer in the English Department in the Fall of 1994, and before that first semester was over our founding editor-in-chief, Richard Peterson met with Allison Joseph, Carolyn Alessio, and me, and we began our initial work figuring how to begin the magazine that became *Crab Orchard Review*. We didn't have funding, a name, or any other staff, but with Allison as poetry editor, Carolyn as prose editor, and me as managing editor, we had an editorial staff and an idea we all four agreed upon—we would pay writers for their work and we have always worked to keep that a part of the magazine. Our first issue of *Crab Orchard Review* appeared in December 1995.

Talk a bit about the long professional relationship and collaboration you've had with your cofounders; I'm guessing you each bring a little something different to the table...

Well, Richard Peterson retired from the SIUC English Department and stepped down as *Crab Orchard Review*'s editor-in-chief in 2001, but he taught me a great deal about the politics and bureaucracy of a university and having the determination to make a project survive and grow despite whatever obstacles are in your way.

Allison Joseph and I have been married now for twenty-two years and, in addition to being the poetry editor of *Crab Orchard Review*, she became our editor-in-chief in 2001. We don't have time for me to begin to describe our relationship—professional and personal—and all I have learned and am still learning from Allison. She is one of the best readers of poetry I have ever met and has a very close eye for what makes an individual poem stand out (or not) in terms of its craft, its phrasing, its music, its imagery, its figurative language, its intelligent and fresh approach to its subject, and how all those elements come together to make the poem memorable and a piece of writing you would want to read again and again. Allison is also devoted to service to other writers and works very hard to share opportunities with other writers through her more than fifteen-year-old free listserve, CRWROPPS, which serves thousands of writers on an almost-daily basis. Our ongoing effort at *Crab Orchard Review* to treat writers the way we would like to be treated ourselves is in large part due to Allison's commitment to that ideal in everything she does.

Carolyn Alessio has been the prose editor of *Crab Orchard Review* since the beginning, and, despite having not been a part of the SIUC English Department for over thirteen years, she continues to provide us with invaluable expertise and insight in her work. Carolyn brought a background in journalism in addition to her own experience as a fiction writer and as a teacher at college and high school. She has taught us all to value the connections made by the prose we publish to the world outside the characters or the writer, and her work with the *Chicago Tribune* as a book reviewer and, in the past as the Deputy Books Editor, have brought a perspective that we feel enriches our fiction and nonfiction prose editorial decisions.

What was your original collective vision for the publication and how has it evolved across time? Who is responsible for the distinctive name?

Besides a commitment to pay *Crab Orchard Review* authors, I think our original collective vision has been pretty consistent over the years. We have always strived to publish the best work we receive that represents the rich possibilities of contemporary writing that can appeal to a general audience of readers.

Allison came up with the name *Crab Orchard Review* by considering the local place names in the region until she arrived upon one that all of us liked. Crab Orchard National Wildlife Refuge is ten minutes from our campus and a major wetlands for migratory birds as they travel south on the Mississippi Flyway.

How about the *CO* Poetry Series? Was it a natural outgrowth of the journal?

The Crab Orchard Series in Poetry grew out an idea I had as a poet who submitted manuscripts of my own for about a decade (at the time) and was often a finalist but never selected for publication. I thought, rather than become bitter or frustrated by this, why not provide an additional venue for publication to strong collections of poetry? Southern Illinois University Press had been very helpful to *Crab Orchard Review* on technical issues when we started the magazine and I was very familiar with the quality of the books they published, so I took the idea of beginning a poetry series to the Director of SIU Press and to his head of Acquisitions. Their main concern was whether we would be able to find collections worthy of publication and I assured them we would have no problem. When we received over six hundred manuscripts for our inaugural competition, they understood what I meant and that has never been a question since.

What follows is the description of the evolution of the Crab Orchard Series in Poetry that we have up online:

The Crab Orchard Award Series in Poetry began in 1998 as a co-publishing venture of *Crab Orchard Review* and Southern Illinois University Press. In 2003, the Crab Orchard Award Series in Poetry changed its name to the Crab Orchard Series in Poetry to reflect a new area in our ongoing project to publish some of the best new work by established and new voices in American poetry. In

addition to continuing to publish our First Book Award and our Open Competition Award winners each year, the series began in 2004 to publish Editor's Selections chosen by the series editor to build upon and expand the strengths of the Crab Orchard Series in Poetry. Editor's Selections are selected from manuscripts submitted to the series editor from authors who are currently published in the Crab Orchard Series in Poetry (who are no longer eligible to enter the Open Competition) or from poets who have already published one or more books who are invited by the series editor to submit a manuscript.

Your *COR* awards for writers are impressive. Share, if you would, a little history in regards to the creation of the various *Crab Orchard* awards and what goes into to selecting recipients.

The awards from *Crab Orchard Review* include our Annual Literary Prizes—the Richard Peterson Poetry Prize, the Jack Dyer Fiction Prize, and the John Guyon Literary Nonfiction Prize—; our Special Issue Feature Awards in Poetry, Fiction, and Literary Nonfiction; and the COR Student Writing Awards—the Allison Joseph Poetry Award, the Charles Johnson Fiction Award, and the Rafael Torch Literary Nonfiction Award. We established these awards over the years to further our goal of seeing literary writers paid as well as we possibly can for their published works.

The first awards given out by *Crab Orchard Review* were the Jack Dyer Fiction Prize and the John Guyon Literary Nonfiction Prize, which we set up at the request of *Crab Orchard Review*'s prose editor, Carolyn Alessio, at the time we entered into our partnership with SIU Press to publish the Crab Orchard Series in Poetry. The press did not feel a prose book series was viable for their list and Carolyn wanted us to find a way to encourage and reward prose writers in some other way since a book prize wasn't going to work for us. Jack Dyer and Dr. John Guyon were among the individuals who made *Crab Orchard Review* possible so we named the prizes in their honor. When our founding editor-in-chief, Dr. Richard Peterson, retired from Southern Illinois University Carbondale (and Allison Joseph took over the position), we added a poetry prize to the two existing literary prizes and named it in his honor. Each year, one winner and at least two finalists are chosen in each category by the editors of *Crab Orchard Review* and the three genre winners are awarded $2,000.00 and published in the next Winter/Spring issue and the finalists are all offered publication and $500.00 if they accept.

The *COR* Student Writing Awards evolved out of the Charles Johnson Awards for Fiction and Poetry, which were founded by former SIUC English Department faculty member Ricardo Cortez Cruz in 1994, the year Allison Joseph and I arrived in Carbondale. After Ricardo left Southern Illinois University, the program languished until Dr. Charles Johnson returned to Carbondale to be honored as a Distinguished Alumnus. I met with him at that time and he asked if *Crab Orchard Review* would be interested in restarting a version of the program in fiction where we would publish the winner and he would provide an award and judge the finalists. From 2005 through 2011, we did that and, when Dr. Johnson retired from the University of Washington, we expanded the project to include poetry and literary nonfiction, naming these awards for our editor-in-chief and poetry editor, Allison Joseph, who donates funds for the awards, and Rafael Torch (August 15, 1975 - December 12, 2011), a gifted and passionate young writer and educator who published the first of his award-winning essays in *Crab Orchard Review*. These award competitions are open to all undergraduate and graduate students who are U.S. citizens or permanent residents currently enrolled (at the time of the submission period) full- or part-time in a U.S. college or university, and the winners now receive $1,000.00 and are published in the next Winter/Spring issue of *Crab Orchard Review*.

The most recent awards added by *Crab Orchard Review* are our Special Issue Feature Awards in Poetry, Fiction, and Literary Nonfiction. These awards are connected to the special thematic issue we do each year and the winners receive $1,500.00 and are published in the Summer/Fall issue that explores that theme. One winner in each genre category—poetry, fiction, and literary nonfiction—is selected by the editors of *Crab Orchard Review*, who are looking for the work in each genre that best embodies the topic of the special issue.

Obviously the SIU Press is a major player in the *Crab Orchard* experience. What role, if any, has your university press had in sustaining and/or promoting excellence in the field of writing (and poetry in particular)?

I have felt so fortunate to work these last fifteen years with SIU Press on the Crab Orchard Series in Poetry. Though literary publishing is not the primary activity of the press (whose focus is more on scholarly publishing in areas that include film and cultural studies, rhetoric and composition, Illinois and, particularly, southern Illinois history, to name a few), the passion that they have shown for publishing the poetry collections, the pride they take in the quality of each book's production, and the support they have shown and continue to show for our authors has been extraordinary.

Of the scores of manuscripts you've edited over the years, is there a collection or project which stands out as particularly memorable or satisfying, or would you say (in general) the creative process is its own reward?

It is very difficult to pick out one collection or project that I have worked on as an editor when there are so many different and rewarding aspects to each one. However, I can say that the experience that has been in many ways the most challenging for me as an editor and has had the greatest impact upon me as a person was this last year's project of shepherding Jake Adam York's collection *Abide* (2014) into print following his death. Jake was a very good friend and I had had the pleasure of really meeting him first through his poems when Cathy Song selected Jake's collection *A Murmuration of Starlings* (2008) as a winner in our 2007 Crab Orchard Series in Poetry Open Competition. Jake's powerful elegies to martyrs of the U.S. Civil Rights Movement that make up this collection changed me as a writer and I admired his work so much that when he told me that there was a companion volume he had completed I went to SIU Press and asked if it would be possible to publish this book, *Persons Unknown* (2010), as well. I am very grateful to SIU Press that they recognized how important it was to publish these books in a way that would emphasize the connection between them and the magnitude of Jake's project to write these elegies, which he called Inscriptions for Air. When Jake emailed me his collection *Abide*, he let me know how much he hoped SIU Press might be interested in doing a third book together but that he also recognized how rare a thing that can be. When I received news of his stroke and death only three days after receiving Abide from him, I was devastated. While still mourning his loss, I read the collection and was deeply moved by the way Jake had continued his Inscriptions for Air project while finding room in the collection to include more of himself as a part of the subject of his poems in a way that deepened the understanding of his readers for the connections Jake made personally to the individuals and events so important to our shared history and to this nation and world. Reading and re-reading Abide, I recognized the great accomplishment Jake had achieved and I began to talk with Jake's family, his colleagues Nicky Beer and Brian Barker, and his wife, Sarah Skeen, about their hopes for the collection and they all confirmed Jake's wish to see the book with SIU Press, if possible. In so many ways, publishing Abide has been a labor of such love, care, and commitment on the part of so many of Jake's friends, his family, and so many of the people at SIU Press and with *Crab Orchard Review* and I know this experience will always be a very important part of me.

What sort of teaching course load are you able to maintain with all of your editing duties? Does it vary from semester to semester, or year to year? Is there any time left to devote to your own writing?

My official job title at Southern Illinois University is "Managing Editor." The work I do on the Crab Orchard Series in Poetry is not even considered to be part of my employment (though I would say it is some of the most rewarding volunteer work I can imagine myself doing). I am available to teach one or two courses in the English Department each year as needed, and I have taught a wide range of composition, literature, and creative writing courses, but there is not a set assignment. I also direct several internships and independent studies each year in a variety of areas of literary publishing.

It is a challenge to find time to devote to my own writing, but I am happier if I do and I think if I am writing I am a better editor so it is worth the effort.

Speaking of which, your poetry has been featured in such publications as *Ploughshares*, *Crazyhorse*, and *Quarterly West*, among others. Are

you one to experiment with any of the myriad of poetry forms, or more comfortable with a less restrictive, fluid style?

> I write in a number of different styles depending upon my purpose. I once wrote a twenty-one poem sequence all about the subject of "Air," each poem in a different form that was created either by Allison Joseph or by me. I write longer narrative poems (200 lines or more) and briefer lyrics (shorter than sonnet length) as well. Most of the time, the poem tells me its form.

Any plans or projects in the works or final thoughts you'd like to share?

> I am currently working to complete two manuscripts that both speak to experiences I had working when I was younger—though in very different situations and I am taking different approaches to the poems to reflect that. I have two other projects in mind to follow these that I'm trying not to think about too much until I have the time and energy to devote to them. That, of course, can be quite a challenge when there is so much to read and so much work to be done, but I wouldn't have that any other way.

It's been a pleasure—thanks so much!

Lark Vernon Timmons
Editor-in-Chief

Reviews

A Girl Goes into the Woods
by Lyn Lifshin

Review by Elizabeth Nichols

Lyn Lifshin's prolific work *A Girl Goes into the Woods* immediately raises the question, what is in the woods? Further, what do the woods represent? Largely autobiographical, Lifshin's collection takes the reader through the anxious tribulations of her childhood and adolescence, culminating in a search for meaning through poetry in adulthood. No subject is off limits for Lifshin. Sexuality and death, traditionally delicate subjects, are boldly explored. In this way, the woods are a place where Lifshin can be herself: where the socially acceptable roles of women are left behind, and the creative spirit flourishes. The first poem in the collection, "But Instead Has Gone into the Woods," introduces the metaphor of the woods in Lifshin's poetry:

> A girl goes into the woods
> and for what reason
> disappears behind the branches
> and is never heard from again.
> We don't really know why,
> she could have gone shopping
> or had lunch with her mother
> but instead has gone into
> woods, alone, without the lover,
> and not for leaves or flowers.
> ...Now you might
> imagine I'm that girl,
> it seems there are reasons. But,
> first consider: I don't live
> very near those trees and my
> head is already wild with branches

The girl leaves the normal, expected patterns of life behind: she refutes the feminine stereotype of shopping. Her reasons are not the ones that society would expect. She is not going into the woods to meet a lover.

Lifshin directly addresses the reader, and challenges the assumption that she is the girl going into the woods. Lifshin's head is already wild with branches: she was always in the woods. She was always part of the woods. And, unlike the girl in the poem, never had a choice of leaving societal norms, but instead never fit into them in the first place. The woods become not so much a physical adventure as much as a mental, inner adventure brimming with discovery.

Lifshin's inner struggles are raw on the page. In her poetry, the body and hair are sources of anxiety, reflection, and ultimately acceptance:

From "Hair"

Later I learned that
what grew out of
the dark where I
couldn't reach
like dreams or
poems was beautiful,
shouldn't be squeezed into,
changed into
something different.
But those years,
apologizing stuffing
that sun-bleached red
under my collar
...never letting it
go where it wanted
...like someone
who couldn't, hadn't
wouldn't admit, didn't
know it had a
life of its own

Trying to conform pained Lifshin. The vibrancy of her being was confined, and she apologized for its wildness. In "Fat," too, Lifshin explores the price of trying to be something other than what one is meant to be: "pressing so hard [into clothes] it / hurt, a punishment squeezing /

myself into / me, into / what I didn't want" (36). One imagines Lifshin's inner self as the woods, full of "dark branches" from years of apologizing and hating who she was (56). It seems that as she accepts her self as firmly rooted the woods, she works through poetry to clear those woods of dark branches and leave only the healthy, loving ones. Indeed, "Fat" and "Hair" are largely representative of Lifshin's poetry: unwilling, and unable to be put in one place, defying expectations, culminating in beauty and understanding.

The collection also spills a lot of ink on the happy, painful, and illusive nature of relationships. Not only between lovers, but also between family and friends. "Things I have," explains Lifshin in "Drifting," "and / don't have / come from this / moving between / people like / smoke". Lifshin becomes ephemeral, passing from one relationship to another, struggling to hold onto and understand the vital moments between people. "Even in the / dream," she continues in "Even There," "every / time I came / close to you / the place that was you / changed to air". These fleeting relationships are also tied to death. Lifshin imagines herself as a corpse in one relationship, and the man she loved as "already dead to / me". Specifically, the image of her mother is especially fleeting and troubled by death:

> From "More Mother and Daughter Photographs"
> ...You can just see
> certain parts of my mother,
> like a branch in a backdrop.
> ...The daughter
> almost blots the mother
> out. It's as if there
> was some huge dark hole
> only a camera would pick
> up where something that
> had got away had been

The mother is reduced to thin branches in the background, overshadowed by the youth of her daughters. She is fragile, barely there. Just as when Lifshin lifts her "Mother to the Commode", and notes that the "hospital bed / could be Everest," and a new phone is line being installed for her mother, but her mother will be "alive less than a week to / use" it. Lifshin looks back on these difficult-to-grasp moments, and makes them permanent, tangible, and chock-full of poetic beauty.

Blood Orange
by Angela Narciso Torres

Review by Elizabeth Nichols

Angela Narciso Torres' *Blood Orange* immerses the reader in the vital sights, sounds, and smells of childhood, family, and living. Torres makes life the "punishing sweet" of a blood orange: ripe, full, and eager to be experienced and understood. The memories of the past hang like fragrant fruit on a tree, waiting to be tasted through Torres' vivid imagery. In Torres' poetry, ephemeral moments find roots and blossom, captured and potent forever. The first poem in the collection, "The Return to San Juan", illustrates this rebirth of the past:

> To know the gaggle of children
> stoning mangoes on Pilar street. To feel
> the white heat of hand rhymes....
> To enter the tile-roofed house....
> ....To hear
> the soft slap of hemp slippers on stone
> when evenings brought the smoke
> of burning leaves.
>
> There was always too much
> To remember of San Juan—summer, a river,
> stories the women sang.

Each sense in engaged in the rediscovery of San Juan. The reader hears the children, feels the heat of hand rhymes, and smells the burning leaves. Memories are alive again and given agency with present-tense verbs: knowing, feeling, and entering in-the-moment. "The Return to San Juan" is a perfect opening to the collection because it signals that, in Torres' poetry, something vital has come back to life and demands to be known.

But, the recapturing of memories and moments in Torres' poetry is not just a way to underline the highlights of the past. There is a sense that the speakers in the collection are searching for meaning; looking for definition in places, in people, and in themselves. With Torres' masterful pen, "We Go Back to Manila in 1999", and roam "through the dark / rooms...rummaging through cupboards and draws, / prowling the backyard rubble to unearth / the stories from which [we] grew". Torres' recollection of her mother in "Lucky" reveals the meaning in the search:

> My mother looks for signs
> on the morning of my departure.
> Everything means something
>
> else, she assures me when
> I topple a juice glass,
> calling it good fortune
>
> when the crystal shatters.

Even the smallest details in life become important—bestow meaning—when they are rediscovered and experienced anew. What was happenstance, or clouded in emotion, becomes a way to understand the present and the self:

> From "Waiting for my Father at the University Hospital Lab"
>
> Clicking against the microscope,
> his ice-cube lenses magnified
> that other universe....
>
> I became infinitesimal, a tight fist
> of fire and constellations, no larger
> than a dust mote on the camera lens
> he polished with a scrap of chamois
> before peering into the deep
> rivers of a heart pinched open.

The poems about her mother and father pin open the hearts of the past, and discover inner lives. The shattering of crystal and the peering of a microscope become pathways into the thoughts and emotions of people in certain moment in time. These two poems, in fact, demonstrate what meaningful, powerful poetry does best: cast a heightened, sharpened lens on life, lending new contrast, color and understanding to everything, even the infinitesimal.

It is especially the vague, and hard-to-pin-down emotions and moments of life that Torres fleshes out beautifully. Life's pauses and fleeting, vibrant bursts transform in the permanency of written poetry into feelings we can access and touch. The intangible becomes tangible:

From "Entre Chien et Loup"

...Anyone

observing how magnolia buds flush
before they speak in white flame

will recognize the wish to linger
...prolonging

that final glimpse, or the urge to pause....

Entre chien et loup, the French say,
implying that all we know of heaven

is in the eyelash between day
and night, between dog and wolf.

The French expression *entre chien et loup* literally translates to between dog and wolf. The expression itself is multi-layered, and Torres' paints each layer of its meaning delicately. Between day and night, that vulnerable time between light and dark, a gray space emerges. In that gray uncertainty, it is impossible to tell a dog from a wolf; to recognize safety from danger. The meaning in life that Torres' speakers search for is shadowed in the between the bright whites of magnolias in the sun, and the blacks of ink and night. In *Blood Orange*, the reader comes closer to the grays of life: feels the uncertainty and makes it known. In the vibrant rediscovery of life and self through poetry, there is a recognition that human existence itself is *entre chien et loup*. Torres' collection assures the reader that with new-found understanding, *"you're found, come home,"*.

Eye to Eye
by Maria Terrone

Review by Elizabeth Nichols

Maria Terrone's *Eye to Eye* is poetic window into human perception. Terrone's collection goes beyond the physical act of sight, and delves into inner world of self-perception. In Terrone's work, "over-ripe vowels / thicken the air," and, through poetry, the reader is led on "a spider's thread to rejoin the human web". In other words, Terrone tackles how we recognize the *human* in others. Further, Terrone investigates how perception is altered through the advent and use of technology, ultimately asking if the human images that technology produces make "shadows" "more real" than flesh and blood. In the end, *Eye to Eye* challenges the way that the reader looks at the world and, therefore, challenges the way that the reader understands the world and themselves.

In the titular poem of the collection, Terrone introduces the major themes in her work. An exhibit note from the Brandywine River Museum that precedes the poem states that, "Toward the end of the 18th century, portraits of the single eye of a loved one became fashionable,". From that exhibit, Terrone describes a moment time in which the human gaze held an almost mystical power:

From "Eye to Eye"

...an eye for an eye. All the rage
in the 18th century: to exchange one of yours
for one of your lover's, to hold the private gaze
beyond the fleeting moment,

so that hazel iris and arched brow,
hint of sideburn or curl can lie
against the other's body for all to see:
love in the eye of every beholder...

With the image of their beloved's eye, the lover has direct access to the inner being of the beloved. The adoration of the beloved is frozen in time, transforming fleeting emotions into a permanent testament of love. In addition, by wearing the portrait, the lover is sharing an intimate piece of their beloved, and having that intimacy reflected back at them in the eyes of those admiring the portrait. The permanency of the portrait creates a never-ending cycle of eyes upon eyes; a climate of shared emotions being pulled into the center of an inner being.

But, is that inner being always correctly perceived? Terrone's vision of the world of ocular portraiture ends with a thought-provoking comparison:

> From "Eye to Eye"
>
> I think of the disentombed—Lazarus emerging
> from the cave, arms raised before that first stab
> of light and piercing stares.
>
> You know how hard it must have been for him
> to live his life again—always those eyes
> riveted on him, wondering what he had seen.

Lazarus tries to protect himself from the piercing power of the human gaze, strong as blinding light. Rising from the dead, the eyes of world ask Lazarus what he saw of the afterlife. Lazarus' life could never return to normalcy, forever wondered at and scrutinized. This contrast to the fist part of the poem demonstrates that even the most penetrating of gazes cannot always spy the mysteries—the inner workings—of a life.

Appropriately, then, Terrone also comments on the physical limitations of sight in "Myopia". Myopia means nearsightedness, or the ability to only see objects near and not far away. Terrone takes this typical physical affliction of the eyes, and gives it emotional depth:

From "Myopia"

> Not a diminishing—
> the body's way of forcing me
> to look closer.
>
> If I lie eye to eye
> with these blades of grass,
> I may see what they hide:
>
> ...maybe the cameo
> that came unpinned
>
> as I walked here decades ago:
> that once noble face
> framed by wild green hair.

The the physical limitations of sight are connected with the intangible ability to see inside ourselves. "Myopia" forces the individual to focus on only what is close. And what could be closer than the inner part of a human being? Unlike looking at a lover's eye, or at Lazarus, the power of the human gaze is turned inward instead of outward. The lesson of Myopia is that we should be looking inside ourselves and not at others to understand the human.

Finally, Terrone addresses the way in which technology changes the way that humanity is perceived. In "A Hologram State of Mind", the hologram Hatsune Miku, a virtual popstar from Japan, "'sings' / synthesized pop in huge stadiums, / bloodless and breathless / for thousands of fans." The audience reacts to the singing hologram the same way that they would react to a flesh and blood singer. Hatsune Miku is not real, but the audience connects with her on a very emotional, human level. Can a hologram teach us to recognize what makes a human, or only serve to blur the lines further between machine and man? The poem concludes:

From "A Hologram State of Mind"

> Today as the self-described
> "philosopher of blogging" lectured,
> the word virtual
> crawled off the the Power Point screen
> over his skin, and I wondered
> if he knew what he saw
> and what we believed was true.

What the poem describes is the lecturer stepping in front of the Power Point screen, and the projection slides across his face instead of the screen. The very word *"virtual"* stamps itself on the lecturer's face. A melding of the human and the virtual has taken place. The speaker in the poem wonders if the lecturer can recognize the difference between the technology and himself. And, further, if the audience listening to the lecturer recognizes that difference. It is key that the lecturer is talking about blogging, which in many cases acts as a virtual record of the blogger's inner most thoughts. Philosophy, the study of understanding what the human being is, has been digitized.

As Terrone points out with the miniature portraits of a lover's eye in the 18th century, the harsh gazes on the resurrected Lazarus, and myopia, looking inside another person—eye to eye—is powerful. Even the digitization of the human gaze, of human thoughts and philosophy, does not diminish its power. The audience still connects on an emotional level with a singing hologram. However, what *Eye to Eye* exists to do, what Terrone's poetry does, is turn the reader's gaze inward. The way to truly understand the self, and what it means to be human, is to look in the mirror eye to eye.

In Both Hands
by Joannie Stangeland

Review by Elizabeth Nichols

In Joannie Stangeland's collection, "In *Both* Hands," "Air becomes written / with messages, / wing echoes, / the days of thin blue paper." Stangeland's poetry is like a waning smoke signal. The message wafting on the wind is difficult to decipher, but well worth the effort. Her deft pen crafts beautiful images of "a moth in silk" and the "day's last glare / like a scarf, silk draped over a paper lampshade." Her poetry is like flowing water running over the psyche, leaving the reader with carefully crafted, potent impressions of joy, fear, anger, and sadness. In Stangeland's poems, it is as if the symbols in our dreams have become tangible, pulsing on the page with fresh-spilled ink. In the midst of these ephemeral images, Stangeland explores the mystery in existence, and the process of writing.

One such mystery explored by Stangeland is the emotional and physical transition from girlhood to womanhood in the poem "In This Myth". Certainly, the physical changes of girlhood to womanhood are scientifically cataloged, but it is much harder (and, arguably much more rewarding) to try and describe the mental and emotional experience of becoming a woman: of describing what being a woman means. "In this myth," the speaker explains, "we are born / through water." And, indeed, the speaker's daughter is described as "More water than bone, / my daughter came out / in a rush, gushing." "Birth," she continues, "is wet. / Desire pushes. I barely remember being a girl." When the speaker admits to barely remembering being a girl, she is not just bemoaning the fading memories of her past, but also sharing her fear with the reader. If she does not remember being a girl, how can she raise her daughter well? Further, and most significantly, the speaker puts these experiences of womanhood into a larger, mythical context:

From "In This Myth"

> I come for sustenance,
> past the surface brilliance—
> depth or heaven.
>
> I never wanted
> to get wet
>
> but to open, to split
> like a pomegranate,
> let all my garnet seeds spill out.

The pomegranate is the key to uncovering Stangeland's reference. While it is colloquially held that in story of Adam and Eve, Eve tempted Adam with an apple, scholars now suggest that the apple was actually a pomegranate. Eve comes to the pomegranate for sustenance of the body and of something she herself cannot define. She never wanted to get wet: never wanted the pain coursing through childbirth. For Eve, transgression was not the point: it was to become fuller, more complex, and full of depth. To be a woman, then, is to know the myths that surround the female being. To be a woman is to uncover the truths and lies in those myths, and to understand the self.

Similarly, in "In Persephone's Wake," Stangeland plumbs the depths of the Greek myth of Persephone and her abduction by Hades into the underworld:

> Again, Persephone leaves
> the common realm before ice veils
> the tree limbs and what grass remains.
>
> …
>
> I curl against her raveling dream,
> look for any watered sunlight
> and watch my own daughter
> carry her stubborn hunger, tempted
> to linger too close to the ground.

Once again, Stangeland uses the myth as a lens through which to discover new meaning in real life. Just as Persephone is drawn to Hades, to the underworld, so too is the speaker's daughter drawn to the ground. The daughter's hunger refers to the seeds that Persephone ate, which rooted her to the underworld. This hunger is not merely an appetite for the transgressive. It is also a hunger for knowledge of the unknown, and ultimately for self discovery. For, as the speaker in the poem reveals, "We think of the goddess [Persephone] as frozen / because she means winter, yet passion burns." Persephone matures, her idle curiosity blossoming into love. Through Stangeland's imagery, there is more at work in unraveling the mysteries of myth and life than meets the eye. What the reader perceives as frozen is instead burning with passion. With the reader would perceive as a story of transgression is instead a story of burgeoning passion and identity.

And, what appear to be "crows" flying the air are actually "words," "oily and stubborn, ruffled and sharp." In many of Stangeland's poems, she comments on and explores the writing process. In the poem, "If I Write the Story Now", she writes, "I'll build this poem over and over, / try to see my future in the lines / the humming bird writes." Interestingly, this 'building of the poem' is framed by myth:

From "If I Write the Story Now"

The myth of my true life emerges—
a pond, fringed by cattails, water a still
eye open to another world....

...

In the myth of my living, our house
is made of time, with windows trimmed in blue,
and I can read the weather coming.

For the speaker, the poem binds the myth together: gives the myth power though imagery. As a poet, the speaker writes her own mythology, defining and empowering her self. In Stangeland's poetry, myths are not only the classic stories retold from tomes. Myths are the stories that inform identity, collecting on the wind and binding together to shape a sense of self. The myth of living is wound tight by symbols, images that tell a collective story: the story of how we are, and how we would like to be. Stangeland pins down the mysteries of existence much like a lepidopterist gently, painstakingly pins down the gossamer wings of a butterfly. The reader is left to bask in the evanescence of life, treasuring the beauty and the power in it.

Moon Over Zabriskie
by Helen Wickes

Review by Leila A. Fortier

I believe it is a fairly accurate assessment to say that most present-day poets are buying and reading two kinds of poetry books: their favorite classics and their friends' books. Through social networking, poets are privy to the creative expressions of peers from all over the world as they swim and commune in shared virtual circles. Chances are, if you have become my friend (meaning that we have shared work or corresponded to some degree), I will purchase and promote your book. I believe this is a highly important task amongst friends and writers, especially in an age where poetry only comprises approximately 1% of the readership market. This essentially means that poets are reading poets and, if you want your work to be read—in all fairness— you really need to read contemporary published poets.

Seemingly gone are the days when we wandered the aisles of the local bookstores, picking through curious, unknown titles and sampling their fresh pages. Do you remember the last time you purchased a book simply because the title or cover was so enticing that you just *had* to read it, even if you knew nothing about the writer? Maybe it would be terrible; maybe it would be *really* good. But, there was a certain rush: a little euphoric nervousness from the impulse of the gamble.

I digress to these moments because I recently fell blissfully prey to marketing I thought had long passed. I was scrolling around in our virtual catalog of announcements, and there were so many new titles, new voices, and new presses. I already purchase books at a faster pace than I can read them. I told myself I was going to slow down. I was trying *not* to pay attention.

From "The Heart Waking Up Braids Her Hair"

But I digress, which is where I found you (42)

Then I saw it: *Moon Over Zabriskie* by Helen Wickes, just released by Glass Lyre Press. My fingers literally paused on the keys as I repeated the title, "*Moon Over Zabriskie...Moon Over Zabriskie...Moon Over....*" The words rolled off my tongue and scintillated. *What is Zabriskie*, I thought? Who is Helen Wickes? Was she one of my friends whose work I had yet to sample? I checked. No. She was completely foreign to me. As I repeated the title I felt my eyes being drawn into the image of a womb-like cave or canyon. The colors and shapes drew me in like a point of entry, and I knew I was about to break my promise. The book was purchased. I felt that same tingle of excitement and anticipation from years ago: would it be terrible or would it be really good? Because we all know that magical feeling when we stumble upon a work that is so good that we feel as though we just unearthed buried treasure.

From "The Heart Waking Up Braids Her Hair"

Sit still, I'm telling you the story
A repertoire of sound spilled at your feet
Language taking aim at the soundless (42)

Maybe I could anticipate what I might be about to read. After all, shouldn't we be introduced first? Poetry is so intimate to me that it seemed only right. So I thumbed to the back of the book where it piqued my interest to discover that Wickes worked many years as a psychotherapist: a subject in which I hold a lot of academic interest. I paused and let my mind wander a bit as I held the slender volume in my hands, wondering if psychoanalysis would influence her writing. I was now ready to begin from the first page with the intention of seeing and experiencing the world through Wickes' eyes:

From "Frost, Then Ice"

Today the whole world is thin ice and we're skating,
giddy with speed,
swerving through rough places,
always about to turn for home,
which is farther than we thought. (46)

As I began to read, I was immediately struck by the visual landscapes of Wickes' words. A quote came to my mind from Russian poet and novelist Boris Pasternak and, I thought to myself, *this* must be who he was writing about: "For a moment she rediscovered the purpose of her life. She was here on earth to grasp the meaning of its wild enchantment and to call each thing by its right name." Confucius also said, "The beginning of wisdom is to call things by their proper name." As I recalled these passages, I was astounded by the truth of them as witness to Wickes' writing. There is no mere word such as 'flower' in Wickes' work, which I surmise would be just as insulting to her landscapes as it would be to speak to people without addressing them by their given names. All elements in her poems speak—*I have a name*—painting ordinary words in fresh-born color and life: pinion cones, juniper, and rye, zinnia and mazanita, laurel and lupine. I am drinking the names of things down to mallow leaf and mesquite. I have entered the honeycomb of the caves and canyons, climbing through "as if it were a body."

From "Titus Canyon"

Wanting to enter the desert. Below the skin.
Come out altered. (88)

I crawl through the canyons, stroll through the valleys, and drink from the Borrego Springs. I am caught within the snapshots of Wickes' experience: her observations, contemplations, and reflections that thread the distant stars into interlaced universes. I have entered nature's canvas. But, I have also entered the shadows of chiaroscuro as I contemplate the meaning behind man's imitations. Wickes' ekphrastic poems unite the artist with the source of inspiration where everything merges. Am I canyon or Caravaggio? But, I do think I saw O'Keefe in every poem: opening with the mouths of caves and zinnia splendor, or the globes of grapefruit releasing their scent beneath the fullness of the moon. Everything in *Moon Over Zabriskie* is expanding and taking in, and only the critic seems separate and out of place now:

From "Another Saturday Night"

>   Raving on. The famous critics say
>   that poems now are all anecdote with epiphany.
>   They'd dislike me. Let them.
>   Right now I'd settle for epiphany,
>   with or without the anecdote.
>
>   When you can't get to the thin edge
>   of your own living, when you can't sharpen it
>   and run barefoot, it hardly seems worthwhile. (67)

On Manannan's Isle
by Usha Kishore

Review by Elizabeth Nichols

Usha Kishore's *On Manannan's Isle* is a poetic exploration of colonization and cultural exchange, and how the two affect personal and national identity. Kishore daringly and beautifully addresses the gulfs between English and Indian culture while simultaneously showing the benefit and the pain of those cultures colliding. *Manannan's Isle* is as much a dialogue between poet and poetry as it is a dialogue between colonized and colonizer. "Any takers?" asks the speaker of the reader in "Culture Trade", inviting public conversation about the emotional and social toll of colonization. "I am not here to invade," assures the speaker, "I only want to trade..." But there is more at work in Kishore's collection than trade: it also encourages the reader to seek understanding and peace. With a deft pen, Kishore weaves spirituality, language, and culture into a stunning example of poetic art, ripe with the richness of life.

Language plays a key role in Kishore's collection, affecting the way in which colonized and colonizer—speaker and reader—understand each other. In "I Emigrate", the speaker explains,

> I shrink from my foster mother-tongue,
> Malayalam, that I never actively learnt,
> but in whose vivid colours I dream

Malayalam gives a different nuance and depth to a subject than English, and the speaker *feels* that difference although she cannot understand her mother-tongue. Malayalam is important to the speaker because it informs and colours her identity. However, English is the language that the speaker is obliged to use, not Malayalam. This creates a complex relationship between English and the speaker:

From "I Emigrate"

> I am colonised by that puzzling paradox,
> English, an alien tongue that I stole
> from my tyrant masters.
>
> I wander the ups and downs of earth,
> an exile with no language of my own.
>
> ...
>
> In the horizon, I meet Poetry...

The English colonized India and, in doing so, made English the 'superior' and 'master' language. The speaker is forced into a space between English and Malayalam, belonging fully to neither language. Her vehicle of expression is compromised; her tongue exiled without language. Yet, the speaker ends the poem with hope. Poetry becomes the language for the exiled.

Further, in "English Teaching", poetry becomes more than just a new vehicle for expression: it becomes power. The speaker boasts, "I have captured / your [the colonizer's] language [English] and coloured her / with my reds, purples and golds." Now, it not only English that colors the speaker's identity, but the speaker who colors English. She takes the power of a language once used to colonize, and uses it for herself:

From "English Teaching"

> History taught me your language
> so that I become you but I remain me.
>
> She [English] has given me
> myself in true colours and dyed
> herself in my silvered metaphors.
>
> She has given me
> her most precious jewel,
> Poetry..."

For the speaker, there is not only power in claiming the language as her own, but also in using the power of English against the colonizer. By 'dying' English in her image, the speaker turns the act of colonization into one of personal and cultural actualization. There is a note of triumph in the speaker's voice, expressing the joy of self-empowerment. And, while English may be used to throw "dagger words," or slurs at her, the speaker uses that same agent of slander and pain to make poetry and beauty. Through poetry, the speaker overcomes the colonizer's "invading imperial tongue," and rechristens English, and her identity, as her own.

Finally, the titular poem of the collection, "On Manannan's Isle", crystallizes the concept of cultural understanding. Kishore weaves the Celtic myth of Manannan, a sea deity, with the "thirty three million gods" of Indian myth. The cultural exile asks of the mystical "voice" rising with tides slamming into the "rugged cliffs," "Vayu? Varuna? Indra? / Which of my thirty three million gods, are you?" The voice answers:

From "On Manannan's Isle"

I am but one more – cloak yourself in my swirling mists,
hear my laughter in the crashing waves, feel my power
in the roaring winds and say my name!

Manannan!
My veg!

Although Manannan is a foreign deity, he claims the exile as his own, calling her "*my veg,*" which is Gaelic for "little one." Manannan is but "one more" god, not a separate entity that can only be a god to one people, one religion. He places himself in a world pantheon of deities, creating a spiritual connection between all belief systems and religions. In doing so, he signals to the exile that she is just as much a part of the Celtic tradition as she is of the Indian tradition. In fact, as Manannan suggests, the two mythos were never separate, at all. The colonizers made the colonized *other* and *lesser* when the two peoples—cultures—were never different. Instead they are connected in the most profound of ways: by the same mythos, the same human spirituality.

Kishore's *On Manannan's Isle* explore colonization and cultural exchange as they concern personal identity. The speaker—the exile—in the collection finds an avenue of power and self-actualization through poetry. She overcomes her colonizers not only through mastery of language, but also through the merging of Celtic and Indian myths. When the speaker would be made other, forced into a pejorative space, she makes a space of her own: a space where English is colored with the cultural colors of India, and the sea deity Manannnan shares spiritual real estate with the Indian deities.

As Manannan explains to the speaker in "Multiculturalism, Postcolonialism...":

> I [Manannan] am the story of the colonised,
> I am the story of the colonial,
> Now, I am your story, your verse.

The experience of cultural exchange, of colonization, of exile, is not isolated to the speaker Kishore's collection. It is instead a human experience, a human story. *On Manannan's Isle* uses the power of poetry to deliver the simplest, if most poignant of ideas: the most important cultural exchange is in recognizing that what is being traded is at heart not different, at all, but equally *human*.

Six Weeks to Yehidah
by Melissa Studdard

Review by Elizabeth Nichols and Royce Hamel

In *Six Weeks to Yehidah*, Melissa Studdard takes the reader on a spiritual journey through the eyes of Annalise of the Verdant Hills. In *Yehida*, "the hold of imagination" becomes as persistent as reality," and Annalise discovers that the journey to discover one's self is also the journey to understanding the human. Despite her young age, Annalise shows the reader the meaning of universal acceptance, encountering strange creatures on her journey but ultimately discovering that people are all "connected...like the strands of a web, each to the other, body to body, mind to mind, heart to heart." With whimsical characters and scenes, the novel calls forth comparisons to *Sophie's World*, *K-PAX*, and *Alice in Wonderland*, but strikes a unique and refreshing note with Studdard's enchanting attention to detail and message of love for the self, and the world.

After a sudden flood washes over the hills where she lives, Annalise finds herself in a cloud. Transported to a spiritual realm, Annalise is tested by the cloud world's inhabitants. Like a hero in a Greek epic, Annalise must pass the tests in order to go home. With her talking sheep friends, Mabel and Mimi, and a guiding light entity, Bob, Annalise travels from one extraordinary locale to another, and tries not only to find a way home, but also to understand and help the creatures she encounters. Annalise creates harmony from discord on Acoustic Island, finds her mother at Hulan House, and guides Mabel and Mimi to their own spiritual pasture. With each test, Annalise understands more and more about herself, and in turn does not leave the cloud world as the same little girl she was before.

Because *Six Weeks to Yehidah* is narrated from Annalise's perspective, the novel breaks down religious and philosophical concepts, and introduces them at a basic level. For example, when Annalise finally finds herself in the city of Yehidah, or the highest plane of the soul, she describes the city as a mandala:

"Each mandala was a big circle or square with smaller designs within. The book [that her mother gave her] explained that the designs mean something, in the same way that words mean something, but that this meaning is understood by a deeper part of our minds than the part that understands words. The book explained that we might understand mandalas without really knowing we understood them."

Annalise admits that she does not understand the book's explanation, but that when she read the book, she felt peaceful. Annalise's experience with her mother's book is the same way that the reader experiences *Six Weeks to Yehidah*. The novel is packed with references to religion and philosophy. A step on the eightfold path of Buddhism is to view reality as it really is, not as it appears to be. As Kana of Hulon House explains to Annalise, "When you traveled the way of the petroglyph, it opened up another eye, and now you see things as they really are, not just how they seem." Although Buddhism is not referenced by name, the reader has just learned about a core tenet of that eastern religion with Annalise. While young readers might not understand all the concepts introduced in the novel, *Yehidah* acts a springboard to spiritual ideas.

There are some who might feel the novel is overly ambitious. References to *The Wizard of Oz*, *The Odyssey*, *Winnie the-Pooh*, and even *Don Quixote*, try and place the novel within a grand literary canon. In addition, the multiple references to different religious and philosophical ideas—up to and including a figure that is called "The Good Shepherd, The Enlightened One, The Light Giving Lamp, The Blessed Virgin, Tara, Krishna—" can often leave the reader asea in a jumble of spirituality. But, as Annalise herself says, there is "No need to define it; Let's just enjoy it." *Yehidah* offers a spirituality of the self rather than a defined theology.

Six Weeks to Yehidah is a beautifully written work with twists and turns that make it a veritable labyrinth of religion and philosophy. Annalise's final task is to learn how she can best contribute, help others, and make the world a better place. Her spiritual journey allowed her to understand herself, and in turn share her wisdom with others. *Yehidah* sparkles with whimsy and rich description while delving into the mysteries of religion and philosophy. In the end, Annalise shows the reader how to become a better person, a better member of the human community through spirit.

The Gathering Light at San Cataldo
by Jeffrey Alfier

Review by Elizabeth Nichols

In *The Gathering Light* at San Cataldo, Jeffrey C. Alfier draws the reader into a world of salt, earth, and human experience with vivid imagery and rich description. Alfier invites the read on a journey by sea, train, and cobbled streets to discover the true depth of Italy: of a historied country and people. Under Alfier's deft guidance and masterful pen, we soon become "Apprenticed to the Sea," speaking "to the wildness of uncertain tides." We share a poet's journey into our common humanity.

The journey begins with the poem "Upon Your Return to Savelletri Harbor". It addresses "vecchio," which is Italian for "old one." The "old one" in this case refers to a wizened elder, perhaps even Italy herself. What is certain is that this address to vecchio is a return, or a regaining, of something vital. The speaker of the poem asks vecchio to "make us known to the sea." For the sea has the power to "summon you [vecchio] out past / the cobbled promenade," and undulate "through your dreams." The sea is interwoven with human life, "causing us to glare at you [vecchio's] bay," and "measure the moon-splashed sea." The speaker is trying to understand the depth of an illusive force and the power it has over human life while vecchio's "prow trolls beyond daydreams of bluefin" and into wisdom. In the last stanza, vecchio heeds the speaker's call, and does return:

From "Upon Your Return to Savelletri Harbor: "

Consider, we pray, vecchio,
...Return, show us your hands,
let them give us their sea.

Vecchio's life is evoked by the sea. It is a life revealed by ebbs and tides. By asking vecchio to show her hands, this poetic evocation suggests a cyclical reciprocity. Just as the sea brings vecchio into sharp relief, so too does vecchio "give us our sea" and breathe vitality and experience into the speaker's life. It is not only vecchio's hands—vecchio's story—that will be revealed on this journey, but the reader's, as well. Vecchio shows the speaker a path to understanding the human experience.

The reader continues with Alfier on this journey as a "vagabondo," a pilgrim on a "passagiata," or light stroll through Italy. In the poem "Passagiata," the *light* stroll is doing more than just take the reader and the speaker through an Italian street: it is illuminating something important.

From "Passagiata"

They [walkers] wade to piazzas from unseen doorways,

...voices melding with thunder that grumbles
down the distant Adriatic to thread the sharp
scents of fried zeppole, frittata and olive wood

fires where old men...
...clutch glasses of wine — red
from grapes rich with the blood-memory

of Vesuvius...."

"Passagiata" is a perfect example of Alfier's expert ability to paint a moment of life and draw the reader into the scene. It is a poem rich in visual imagery, sounds, and scents. The reader shares in the speak experience of the thunder of the sea, smoky fire and sweet food, and taste of wine. Yet, with the "blood-memory of Vesuvius," there is an undercurrent of lingering memories in the minds of the walkers. The land itself, as well as the people, remembers the tragedies and triumphs of the past. The passagiata, illuminates Alfier in the footnote, is "an early evening ritual in Italy where town folk emerge...to meet with friends...to share each other's world." What the reader is sharing with the speaker and the poet, then, is the world of Italy and her people. The reader physically experiences the country, and emotionally resonates with the people. In Alfier's "Passagiata," human life melds so seamlessly into its physical surroundings that what appears to be a simple walk becomes a way to feel another human life.

Alfier's journey through the emotional, historical, and physical landscapes of Italy comes to a touching close with "The Paving Stones:"

> When the street was found, I shook her [the contadina's] hand
> warm as hearthstones, smelled the wild
> chicory and figs she's picked that morning
> near the sea....

Once again, Alfier makes the scene tangible to the reader through touch and sent. And, here, at the end of the journey, the footsteps of the speaker and the poet have also become the reader's steps. Just as vecchio revealed her hands at the outset of the collection, so too does the contadina, or "Italian peasant woman." But, while vecchio only showed the reader the way to human experience and understanding, the contadina shakes hands with the speaker/reader, signaling that Italy and her people have "grown less remote and foreign now." The country and the people are no longer verses and images on Alfier's pages, but fleshed out and feeling human beings. Further, the speaker asks the contadina,

> ..."Signorina, come si dice [how do you say]:
> Do I still remain a stranger in your eyes?"
> She said I could now find alone
> any street I'd never been down."

Not only has the speaker ceased to be a stranger to the contadina, he has also ceased to be a stranger to the shared humanity between them. The speaker and the reader traveled through the vistas of Italy on a revival of the human spirit in *The Gathering Light at San Cataldo* and, now—taking the hands of vecchio, the contadina, the poet, and the people of Italy—have the ability to discover the heart and beauty of strangers and strange lands. Who, shows Alfier, were never really strangers to begin with.

The Map of What Happened
by Susan Elbe

Review by Elizabeth Nichols

Susan Elbe's *The Map of What Happened* poetically reveals the human aspect of the iron jungle, specifically the city of Chicago. Elbe's collection not only describes the Great Chicago Fire and the Union Stockyards, but also gives those historic events and places human perspective and emotion. If *The Map of What Happened* in Chicago is a static line of events, and the human memory of the city and its past is hazy, then Elbe makes that static line a live wire that crackles and spits with life, fleshing out raw and powerful moments in time. Elbe's masterful pen puts the reader in Chicago—puts Chicago in the reader—with evocative imagery and word play. In the end, Elbe's poetry shares the sorrows, secrets, and lives of Chicagoans and their city, creating a map of humanity.

Elbe's collection opens with the poem "Coda: The City Says". In it, the city of Chicago is given a voice, and speaks directly to the reader:

From "Coda: The City Says"

.... I'm your nerve and and your jugular,
your bullet and needle,
      your gangster and gangway

holler, the sweet home guitar
you rub bottleneck blues up against.

Chicago becomes as much of a character as its inhabitants. The people do not merely live in Chicago, but are defined by Chicago, and in its gritty physicality share an identity. "You'll swear you'll never come back," the city says, "but I'm who you won't leave." Indeed, as the collection progresses, Elbe reveals that it is impossible to leave the city—the past—behind, because it shapes, and is shaped by, its people.

Similarly, the poem "With a Leaf in Her Fist" demonstrates that even in the remote reaches of history, it was (and is) the human that defines a moment. The poem opens with a idyllic perception of life in the city:

From "With a Leaf in Her Fist"

...delighted they said in everything—

> September's buttermilk sky,
> summer's breakdown
> swinging manic throughout
> the Trees of Heaven,
> the light,
>
> everything about the light.

This bright, innocuous light transforms into "the oil stove's flame," "black butterflies, and "The burning." The infamous tale of the start of the Great Chicago Fire is conveyed through simple images. The delighted speaker at the beginning of the poem is forever changed by the horror of the fire, and asks the reader, "Do they bury the dead without shoes? / Do they stitch their mouths shut?" The identity that the speaker possessed at the beginning of the poem vanishes, burned with the fire: "I'm going up / in smoke." In Elbe's poem, the Great Chicago Fire is no longer an isolated historical incident, frozen in time. Instead, a vision of normalcy is put before the tragedy of the fire, and the reader is made to feel the unforgiving speed with which human life can change irrevocably.

But, Elbe is not content to only give voice to the past. "Look," says the speaker in the poem "The Map of What Happened", "it wasn't only death that pushed me down." In other words, it was not just one, isolated incident that defined the speaker's identity. Instead, "It was was the bridge from there to here:" the map of what happened—the whole story of a life. But, what power is there in tracing the roads traveled? In discovering how an identity is born? The speaker answers:

From "The Map of What Happened:"

> ...proof I only belonged to myself:
>
>   the door to a dismantled house I wore
>   like a scapular beneath my blouse,
>
> two cicadas singing in my suitcase,
>
> and this thin-skinned map.
>
> I've carried them with me everywhere
> hoping someday to be found.

The speaker does not simply leave behind the places that shaped her identity, but carries them with her. By wearing the door beneath her blouse, the speaker is taking ownership of what defines her. She makes the memories—and the places that shaped her—her own. It is in this way that she only belongs to herself: she finds power in tracing the roots of her identity.

Finally, Elbe closes the collection with the poem "Will Come Back". The very title of the poem brings the collection full circle by echoing the voice of Chicago in "Coda: The City Says:" "I'm who you won't leave." After breathing in the "stink that meant work" wafting from the Stockyards—after feeling the emotional heat of the Great Chicago Fire—after having "nightmares / about The [atomic] Bomb"—"this," says the speaker in "Will Come Back," "is how we will come back:" "slouching / through the night... / eyes burning for the past." The speaker continues:

From "Will Come Back"

> We'll come back, backyard sparrows looking for stale
> bread, but won't recognize what the heart's held dear,
> stewed down to factory steam, the glitter of black
> gutter-silt.

Time distorts memory. What the speaker remembered, expected to find, is transformed, grossly different. But, this does not mean that tracing the past, tracing the origins of identity and the city of Chicago, was in vain. When Elbe says, "come back," she is saying that we need to do more than just look at static maps, and dry histories that are bereft of the human experience. We need to do more than just treat memories as fading images that lose depth and poignancy with time. Coming back means making *The Map of What Happened* in life personal, emotional, and tangible. Coming back means finding our selves, whether we are ready for it, or not—whether we recognize the person we find, or not. Certainly, the city—Chicago—is ready for its people to find themselves in its iron jungle, again.

Woman in Metaphor: An Anthology of Poems Inspired by the Paintings of Stephen Linsteadt
Edited by Maria Elena B. Mahler

Review by Elizabeth Nichols

Woman in Metaphor: An Anthology of Poems Inspired by the Paintings of Stephen Linsteadt continues the artistic search for universal human truth through the figure of a woman. The collection is a beautiful marriage of the arts: painting and poetry inspire self-reflection through the feminine. Stephen Linsteadt's art of ghostly, often faceless, women evokes a poetic exploration that translates not only the optical expression of his paintings, but more importantly the emotional response evoked by them. These women inhabit spaces that are at once familiar and otherworldly, provoking the poet to explore "what lies beneath our surface," and "draw us closer to the nonphysical world." At heart, the collection is a search for the inner self, and draws on the simultaneously deified, earthly, virginal, sexual, physical, metaphysical woman whose image serves as a timeless metaphor of life. "The metaphor," explains Lois P. Jones in the foreword, "which can be found in womankind, exists as the deific confirmation of an ideology who renews with every season and every birth." In other words, the woman is an ideological vehicle for art and life: she is renewal, birth, and the wellspring of our selves.

The first image of woman in the collection is an obscured, disjointed one. Entitled "Amorous Games in a Flower Garden," Linsteadt's painting reveals only glimpses of a woman. Her head is surrounded by thick strokes of black, the words beside it more prominent than her blurry, smeared face. Her gray eye stares at the viewer. Her exposed chest is pushed forward by invisible, whited-out arms. Her lips are a red punch of color: a suggestion, an invitation of meaning. The first poem by Russell Thorburn parses out this meaning; this intangible emotion:

From "One Week Last Summer"

I am hung at the side somewhere, my hand
about to pulse up with some misunderstanding,
about to yield to the petals
at her breasts, a hand to reach out

before her roundness meets a thorn.

The speaker sets himself a part from the photograph/painting of the woman. Yet, even as he distances himself from her petals—her bloom of open beauty and sexuality—he reaches for her. The speaker in the poem not only wants a physical confirmation of the woman, not only has a desire for her, but wants to capture the moment. He wants to hold onto the effervescent feeling that the woman evokes, much the way that Linsteadt's painting does. In a way, the speaker becomes an artist like Linsteadt: compelled by transcendent beauty to preserve, create. Indeed, in the last line, the speaker suggests that if he does not capture the image of the woman, her image will become marred by a thorn. There is a sense that something will inevitably destroy this moment; that it will become less perfect, less potent if not captured. Thorburn's speaker ultimately raises a question that guides the rest of the collection: is desire for the woman, or what she represents, stronger?

Lia Brooks' poem, "War", picks up the question. Her poem is prefaced by Linsteadt's painting, *The Unknown Woman*. The woman in the painting is the very essence of the unknown: her head is cut off, her face and immediate identity disrupted. The only part of the woman that the viewer sees is her askew torso. Her ribs and breasts are prominent. One might think that Linsteadt has left the woman be to be objectified, but that is far from the truth. Rather, as in Brooks' poem, the body of the woman is meant to represent something that transcends the physical:

From "War"

you have watched the indent in the earth
where the air raid shelter was removed

by those difficult men

who left their eyes on you too long

...so you return then
to the room, find it quiet

and morning, slipping through the curtains
onto your open dressing-gown,

no longer something that ushers
war; each touch the weight of a spider

cool on the skin as your back arches
the flush spreads across a body

that any man would find complete.

Here, the nameless something that Thorburn's speaker was trying to capture has a name: normalcy. During war, much like Thorburn's speaker, the men left their eyes on the woman too long, drawn to her physicality. After the horrors of the war, the body of the woman represents a return to order. In her body, there is a renewal of life. In her body, there is the making of a family; the cornerstone of society. She represents what was lost due to war, and is also the vehicle by which what was lost will be regained.

But, as Lois P. Jones suggested in the foreword, perhaps what the woman really embodies is beyond words, beyond the tangible. Linsteadt's own painting, *Beyond Words*, shows the viewer a blurred form of a woman, pressing up against a surface full of words that obscure her. She is trying to be seen, but all the viewer can make out are the words held up against her body. This stymied perception is not just one-way. Just as the viewer's image of the woman is blurred and labeled, so too is the woman's perception of her self blurred and labeled as she looks back at the world. Lois P. Jones' poem, "Beyond Words," pays homage to this obscured woman by giving her a voice: "Words erase me. / They unmake the bed of me and you lie in it imagining." When the viewer imagines a woman, sees her, he cannot see what she actually is, but what he *believes* she should be. He cannot grasp what she represents, because words tell him what she is *supposed* to be. Jones' speaker goes further:

From "Beyond Words"

Words were built for a deaf God.
Let's be silent, blind and fingerless the way love is.
Knowing what goes beyond the visible, the tangible–
it says I am real, it says don't think. The more we speak

the more our dialect changes until we barely understand.
We never had to learn a language in the dark.

The speaker, the obscured woman, challenges her viewer. She challenges the viewer to forgo language that is heavy with preconceived notions. Without language, a deaf God has no choice but to rely on sight, sound, smell, touch: to experience the truth of the world without filters. The speaker takes away another sense—sight—and the viewer is closed off from the outside world. The viewer has all vehicles of preconception taken away, and is forced to experience the woman in the dark. In order to truly understand the woman, what she represents, the viewer is tuned into the inner world of the intangible.

It is as Stephen Linsteadt concludes in his own poetic work, "Both Sides of Beauty:" "I lay and wait for the cunning huntress / to turn me inwards upon myself." Physical beauty is not all that the feminine offers the artist. Rather, the female figure offers something much more fleeting and powerful: a sense of the human, a sense of self. While the woman in Thorburn's poem suggests sexuality, and the woman in Brooks' poem represents order, the woman in Jones' poem only gives the viewer her *self*. The fragmented, blurred images of women that Linsteadt's paintings present remove the traditional messages of sexuality and motherhood. Instead, what Linsteadt, and *Woman in Metaphor* offer is the inner world of female and, in doing so, bring the reader closer to the inner world of humanity: without body, without artifice. Most of all, this collection shows that the female figure in art is not static, but very much alive and brimming with the possibility to discover our selves.

Developing a Photograph of God
by Robert S. King

Review by Karen Bowles

Robert. S. King has given his readers a glimpse into the divine essence of poetry in his new collection *Developing a Photograph of God*. His stirring imagery takes readers on a journey through the peaks and valleys of the human heart, set against the backdrop of nature. King takes many guises in his storytelling, including that of the best-known fallen seraph, who reminds us that "the voice of an angel / cannot be burned." King's voice sears his words into the imagination of his audience:

From "Eve Bears All She Knows"

> Now we both know that life burns us alive,
> know the bitter aftertaste of sweet fruit's ash,
> hear strange passions blowing around us,
> flutes of hollow trees played by wind, a voice
> rising from the snake or God—
> which one we cannot always tell.

King repeats iconic symbols throughout his work: storms, snakes, stones, hearts. Readers can draw parables from each as a tapestry of titanic struggle is woven, detailing the big and small events that come together to create a life. He reminds readers that to be vulnerable does not mean one is simply breakable; being open to the difficult events in life can reveal that every seeming stone contains a pulsing heart that burns with the heat and light of many suns. In short, it is the energy coursing through every human heartbeat:

From "River Pulse"

> smoothed by wear
> in any panned stream is a load of stones
>
> call them eggs that never hatched
>
> call one a heart too hard to break
> that keeps the river flowing

King does not keep his words corralled into any small piece of Heaven or Earth, but eschews boundaries, drawing a map without the usual reference points, where he "removed all the borders, / erased the points of power." This expansive poetic cosmos is open to all: "Nothing anywhere is native, / but everything belongs." While King poses many questions about universal matters in both a literal and figurative sense, he does not shy away from the ultimate possibility that the great revelations and answers are not yet to be ours, if ever:

From "The Children of Chaos"

> Through any scope
> everything is a matter of importance
> that explodes, collides, merges—super
> novae and black holes stirred in a soup
> rising to the boil of another journey,
> attracted by the gravity of elsewhere.

Reader and writer are all intrepid explorers in King's world. As each individual goes about their unique journey, King reminds us of the larger expedition that we are all on together. Each glimpse we take of either the soil beneath our feet or the stars looming above our head is special enough to be a "Photograph of God."

King's steady voice throughout each poem in his collection may sometimes veer between slightly weary to weatherbeaten and time-tested strength, but his stance seems to always be, at its heart, that of the willing adventurer who will not be daunted by qualms or unanswered queries. He will carry on searching, and asks that we do no less:

From "Explorer"

> Wind imposes its will
> in my motheaten but seaworthy sail.
> On an ocean of sorrow and regret,
> the gales of hope and fear howl
> together toward an unknown shore.

Publication Credits

Jane Hirshfield	"Zero Plus Anything Is A World" First appeared in *Poetry London* "Ordinary Rain. Every Leaf Is Wet" First Appeared in *Five Points* "I Cast My Hook. I Decide To Make Peace" First appeared in *American Poetry Review* "Mop Without Stick" First appeared in *Ploughshares*
Cin Hochman	"Insomnia" First appeared in *The Stray Branch* and *Levure Littéraire*
Lois P. Jones	"The Landscape of Flight" Appeared in the anthology, *The Poet's Quest for God*, Eyewear, April 2014.
Melissa Studdard	"The Universe" From *I Ate the Cosmos for Breakfast*, Saint Julian Press, September 2014
Jon Tribble	"The Scarab's Tracks" First appeared in *Contemporary Voices: A Journal of Poetry*, April 2012.

Contributor Notes

Jeffrey Alfier is the author of *The Wolf Yearling* (Silver Birch Press), *Idyll for a Vanishing River* (Glass Lyre Press) and *Terminal Island: Los Angeles Poems* (Night Ballet Press, forthcoming). His recent work appears or is forthcoming in *Spoon River Poetry Review, New York Quarterly* and *Tulane Review*.

Francesca Bell's poems have appeared in many journals, including *Rattle, burntdistrict, North American Review, Passages North, Poetry Northwest*, and *Gargoyle*. New work is forthcoming in *River Styx, Crab Creek Review* (her poem was a finalist in their recent contest), *Flycatcher*, and *Tar River Poetry*. She has been nominated six times for the Pushcart Prize. Her full-length manuscript was a finalist in the Poetry Foundation's 2012 Emily Dickinson First Book Award competition, a finalist in Carnegie Mellon Press's 2013 open submission period, a semi-finalist for the 2012 and 2013 Philip Levine Poetry Prize, and a finalist for the 2013 May Swenson Poetry Award.

Laboni Bhattacharya is almost done with her Masters in Literature at Delhi University. She takes an inordinate amount of pleasure in traveling, reading fanfiction, birdwatching and sleeping. She also writes whenever she can overcome a crippling anxiety of influence.

Laurie Byro's short stories and poetry have appeared in a dozen or so small presses. Additionally, her work has been published in *The Literary Review, Single Parent, Redactions, Sonnetto Poesia, Chaminade Review, Chronogram, Grasslimb, Re:al Journal, The New Jersey Journal of Poets, Red Rock Review, The Paterson Literary Review,* and *the 7th Quarry* among others. Her work can be googled on-line and in the *Guardian Unlimited* workshop. She was thrice nominated for "The Pushcart Prize" and has won or placed in 39 IBPC competitions. In January 2011, Laurie was named "Poet of the Decade" by the IBPC competition for her 2000-2010 work. Her work was recently published in *The Poetry of Place Anthology* (honoring William Carlos Williams) and the *American Dream Anthology*. Her children's poem "A Captain's Cat" has appeared in *Cricket Magazine* and a textbook *Measuring up to the Illinois Learning Standards*. Her first book *The Bird Artists* was published in 2009 and Laurie was proclaimed as the "Official Poet Laureate of Allendale, NJ." Her work draws on myth and fairytale and her experiences of foreign places in the years she worked as a travel agent. Her poetry insists upon the continuing importance of fantasy, mystery and "the other" in our lives. Laurie facilitated "Circle of Voices" at libraries in New Jersey for over 16 years.

Hélène Cardona is a poet, linguist, dream analyst, author of *Dreaming My Animal Selves* (Salmon Poetry), winner of the Pinnacle Book Award and the 2014 Readers' Favorite Award in Poetry; *The Astonished Universe* (Red Hen Press); and *Life in Suspension*, forthcoming from Salmon Poetry in 2016. *Ce que nous portons* (Éditions du Cygne), her translation of *What We Carry* by Dorianne Laux, came out in September 2014. She also translated *Beyond Elsewhere* by Gabriel Arnou-Laujeac. Hélène holds a Masters in English & American Literature from the Sorbonne, taught at Hamilton College & Loyola Marymount University, and received fellowships from the Goethe-Institut & Universidad Internacional de Andalucía. She is Main Editor of *Dublin Poetry Review* and *Levure Littéraire*, and a multiple-time Pushcart Prize and Best of the Net nominee. Other publications include *Washington Square, World Literature Today, Poetry International, The Warwick Review, The Dublin Review of Books, The Irish Literary Times, The Los Angeles Review*, and many more. Acting credits include *Chocolat, Dawn of the Planet of the Apes, The Hundred-Foot Journey*, etc. For *Serendipity*, she co-wrote with director Peter Chelsom and composer Alan Silvestri the song *Lucienne*, which she also sang.

Kelly Cherry has published 22 books (novels, stories, poetry, essay, memoir), 9 chapbooks, and 2 translations of classical drama. Her most recent book of poetry is *The Life and Death of Poetry* (LSU, March 2014), and *A Kind of Dream*, a collection of interlinked stories, is forthcoming this spring. Next fall will see publication of *A Kelly Cherry Reader*. She lives with her husband in Halifax, Virginia.

Lisa J. Cihlar's poems have appeared in *Blackbird, South Dakota Review, Green Mountains Review, Crab Creek Review,* and *Southern Humanities Review*. She has been twice nominated for a Pushcart Prize and was also a Best of the Net nominee. Her chapbook, *The Insomniac's House*, is available from Dancing Girl Press and a second chapbook, *This is How She Fails*, is available from Crisis Chronicles Press. She won the Blue Light Press chapbook contest and her chapbook, *When I Pick Up My Wings from the Dry Cleaner*, will be published in 2014. She lives in rural southern Wisconsin.

Tobi Cogswell is a multiple Pushcart nominee and a Best of the Net nominee. Credits include or are forthcoming in various journals in the US, UK, Sweden and Australia. In 2012 and 2013 she was short-listed for the Fermoy International Poetry Festival. In 2013 she received Honorable Mention for the Rachel Sherwood Poetry Prize. Her sixth and latest chapbook is *Lapses & Absences*, (Blue Horse Press). She is the co-editor of the *San Pedro River Review* (www.sprreview.com).

Joan Colby has published widely in journals such as *Poetry, Atlanta Review, South Dakota Review, The Spoon River Poetry Review, New York Quarterly, the new renaissance, Grand Street, Epoch,* and *Prairie Schooner.* Awards include two Illinois Arts Council Literary Awards, *Rhino* Poetry Award, *the new renaissance* Award for Poetry, and an Illinois Arts Council Fellowship in Literature. She was a finalist in the GSU Poetry Contest (2007), *Nimrod International* Pablo Neruda Prize (2009, 2012), and received honorable mentions in the *North American Review's* James Hearst Poetry Contest (2008, 2010). She is the editor of *Illinois Racing News*, and lives on a small horse farm in Northern Illinois. She has published 11 books including *The Lonely Hearts Killers, The Atrocity Book* and her newest books from Future Cycle Press—*Dead Horses* and *Selected Poems. Selected Poems* received the 2013 FutureCycle Prize. A chapbook, *Bittersweet*, is forthcoming from Main Street Rag Press in 2014.

Rachel Abramson Dacus is a poet and dramatist whose works include the poetry books *Earth Lessons* and *Femme au Chapeau*, as well the recent *Gods of Water and Air*, a collection of poetry, prose, and drama. She has written on a variety of subjects, from travel in Italy to growing up a rocket scientist's daughter during the race-to-space Cold War era. Her poems, stories, essays, reviews, plays and interviews have appeared in *Atlanta Review, Boulevard, Prairie Schooner, Rattapallax*, and many other journals. She is at work on *The Impresario*, a drama about the great Baroque sculptor Gian Lorenzo Bernini. She lives in Walnut Creek, California and raises funds for nonprofit organizations. Read more at http://racheldacus.net.

J.P. Dancing Bear is editor for the *American Poetry Journal* and *Dream Horse Press*. Bear also hosts the weekly hour-long poetry show, *Out of Our Minds*, on public station, KKUP and available as podcasts. He is the author of thirteen collections of poetry, his latest book is *Love is a Burning*

Building (FutureCycle Press, 2014). His work has appeared, or will shortly, in *American Literary Review*, the 2014 *Poet's Market* and elsewhere.

Peggy Dobreer came to poetry by way of dance and experimental theater. A career artist and educator, she believes that figs are the flushest fruit, and tango is absolutely necessary. Her first book of poetry, *In The Lake of Your Bones*, was published in 2012 by MoonTide Press. Individual poems have been published in *Malpais Review, Fogged Clarity, L.A. Yoga Magazine, The Bicycle Review,* and Matthew Mars' Haiku Remix Project. In 2013, Ms. Dobreer was included in the anthologies *A Poet Is a Poet No Matter How Tall*, edited by Raundi Kai Moore-Kondo and *Ekphrastia Gone Wild*, edited by Rick Lupert, which also featured the work of Nobel Laureate Wislawa Szymborska. Peggy is a member of Beyond Baroque Literary Arts Center and has been interviewed for *Poets Cafe* by Lois P. Jones. She lives in Los Angeles with her daughter. You may visit her at www.peggydobreer.com.

Bruce Louis Dodson has recently relocated from Seattle, Washington, to Borlänge, Sweden, where he continues to practice photography and write fiction and poetry. Some of his most recent work has appeared in: *Breadline Press West Coast Poetry Anthology, Foreign & Far Away – Writers Abroad Anthology, Sleeping Cat Books – Trip of a Lifetime Anthology, Sounds of Solace – Meditative Verse Anthology, The Crucible, The Path, Barely South Review, 3rd Wednesday,* and *Northern Liberties Review.*

Howard Faerstein's first book of poetry, *Dreaming of the Rain in Brooklyn*, a selection of the Silver Concho Poetry Series, was published in 2013 by Press 53. His poetry has appeared in numerous journals; recent publications include *Great River Review, Nimrod, CutThroat, Off the Coast, The Comstock Review, Mudfish* and on-line in *Gris-Gris,* and *Connotation.* Faerstein is assistant poetry editor for *CUTTHROAT, A JOURNAL OF THE ARTS.* He lives in Florence, Massachusetts, and teaches American Literature at Westfield State University.

Ricky Garni is a writer and designer living in North Carolina. He is presently completing a collection of tiny (I mean, these are teensy tiny!) poems entitled *WHAT'S THAT ABOUT,* dutifully banged out on Faye Hunter's 1971 Smith Corona typewriter in purple cursive typeset, and dedicated with great affection to her memory.

Ralph Hamilton is the editor of *RHINO*. With an MFA in poetry from Bennington College, his poems have appeared in a number of journals including *Court Green, Cut Bank* and *Blackbird*. His first book of poems, *Subtle Knot*, will be published in 2015 by Sibling Rivalry Press. Until recently Ralph sat on the board of the Ragdale Foundation. Additionally, he served as judge for *Fifth Wednesday Journal's* (FWJ) winter poetry prize, judged NWCC 2014 poetry prize, and is currently the guest poetry editor for *FWJ's* Fall issue.

Until 2003, **David M. Harris** had never lived more than fifty miles from New York City. Since then he has moved to Tennessee, married, acquired a daughter and a classic MG, and got serious about poetry. All these projects seem to be working out pretty well. His work has appeared in *Pirene's Fountain* (and in the *Best of Pirene's Fountain* anthology), *Gargoyle, The Labletter, The Pedestal*, and other places. His first collection of poetry, *The Review Mirror*, was published by Unsolicited Press in September, 2013. On Sunday mornings, at 11 AM Central time, he talks about poetry on WRFN-LP in Pasquo, TN (www.radiofreenashville.org).

Meg Harris is a writer and a teacher. A graduate of Vermont College of Fine Art, Meg's short stories, essays, and poems have appeared in both print and online journals: *Whiskey Island, The Cafe Review, Upstreet,* and others. Her chapbook of poems, *Inquiry into Loneliness* is forthcoming from Crisis Chronicles Press this year and she has work forthcoming in *The Tower Journal*. Meg serves as one of three judges for Goodreads' monthly poetry contest. She lives with her family in New England.

Jane Hirshfield's poetry speaks to the central issues of human existence—desire and loss, impermanence and beauty, the many dimensions of our connection with others and the wider community of creatures and objects with which we share our lives. Demonstrating with quiet authority what it means to awaken into the full capacities of attention, her work sets forth a hard-won affirmation of our human fate. Described by The New York Times as "radiant and passionate" and by other reviewers as "ethically aware," "insightful and eloquent," and as conveying "succinct wisdom," her subjects range from the metaphysical and passionate to the political, ecological, and scientific to subtle unfoldings of daily life and experience. Her book of essays on the "mind of poetry" and several anthologies recording the work of women poets from the past have become classics in their fields. An intimate, profound, and generous master of her art, Hirshfield has taught at UC Berkeley, Duke University, Bennington College and elsewhere, and her many appearances at writers conferences and literary festivals in this country and abroad have been highly acclaimed.

Jane Hirshfield is the author of seven collections of poetry, including the new *Come, Thief*, published in August 2011, After (shortlisted for England's T.S. Eliot Prize and named a "best book of 2006" by the *Washington Post, the San Francisco Chronicle*, and the *London Financial Times*), *Given Sugar, Given Salt* (finalist for the 2001 National Book Critics Circle Award), *The Lives of the Heart*, and *The October Palace*, as well as a book of essays, *Nine Gates: Entering the Mind of Poetry*. She also edited and co-translated four books containing the work of poets from the past: *The Ink Dark Moon: Love Poems by Komachi & Shikibu, Women of the Ancient Court of Japan, Women in Praise of the Sacred: 43 Centuries of Spiritual Poetry by Women, Mirabai: Ecstatic Poems*, and *The Heart of Haiku*, on Basho, named an Amazon Best Book of 2011. Her work appears in the 2013 editions of *The Best Spiritual Writing, The Best American Poetry*, and *The Pushcart Prize Anthology*. Hirshfield is currently working on a new book of poetry titled *The Beauty*, and a book of essays titled *Ten Windows: How Great Poems Transform the World*, both to be released in 2015.

Hirshfield's other honors include The Poetry Center Book Award; fellowships from the Guggenheim and Rockefeller Foundations, the National Endowment for the Arts, and the Academy of American Poets; Columbia University's Translation Center Award; and (both twice) the Commonwealth Club's California Book Award and the Northern California Book Reviewers Award. In 2012 she received the Donald Hall-Jane Kenyon Prize in American Poetry.

Hirshfield's work has appeared in *The New Yorker, The Atlantic, The Times Literary Supplement, The Nation, Orion, The American Poetry Review, Poetry*, seven editions of *The Best American Poetry*, four *Pushcart Prize Anthologies*, and many other publications. Her work frequently appears on Garrison Keillor's public radio *Writer's Almanac* program and has also been featured in two Bill Moyers PBS programs. In fall 2004, Jane Hirshfield was awarded the 70th Academy Fellowship for distinguished poetic achievement by The Academy of American Poets, an honor formerly held by such poets as Robert Frost, Ezra Pound, William Carlos Williams, and Elizabeth Bishop. In 2012, she was elected a Chancellor of the Academy.

Melinda B. Hipple is an award-winning artist, photographer and writer. Her published works have appeared in *Hillock, Prune Juice, Haijinx, Notes from the Gean, Tinywords* and *Linx*, and she has been a regular contributor to *Pirene's Fountain*. Three of her poems were selected for *First Water*, a *Pirene's Fountain* anthology. She was a past editor and columnist for *Up the Creek News*, and from September 2009 through June 2011 was haiga editor and web master for *Notes from the Gean*, a journal of Japanese short form poetry. She was a founding member and haiga editor for *A Hundred Gourds*, a haikai poetry journal. Melinda has now gone back to school to finish what she started forty years ago. In 2013 she was inducted into Sigma Tau Delta, the international English honor society.

Cin Hochman, from Brooklyn, New York, is the president of Harrison/Hochman "100 Proof " (proofreading/editing services) and the editor-in-chief of the online journal *First Literary Review-East*. She is on the book review staff of *Pedestal* magazine and writes reviews for *Home Planet News* and many other journals. Recent and forthcoming poetry publications include *Arsenic Lobster, Lips, CLWN WR, the Long Islander*, and *MonkeyBicycle*. Her chapbook, *The Carcinogenic Bride*, is on the "Recommended List" of Winning Writers.

Claire Ibarra is a writer, poet and photographer residing in Miami, Florida. Her poetry has appeared in *Thrush Poetry Journal, Blue Fifth Review, Words Dance,* and *Lummox 2*, among others. She is also a contributor to the anthology *Point Mass* by Kind of a Hurricane Press.

RJ Jeffreys is a published poet, writer and playwright, associate editor for the *Tiferet Journal*, featured blogger, editorial and book consultant, writing coach and host of the popular *The Write Step with RJ Jeffreys* radio interview show. Jeffreys' WriteStep blog is featured by Networkedblogs.com as a top ten website for writing advice.

RJ Jeffreys work has appeared in numerous publications, media outlets and websites such as Mass Poetry.org, the *Tiferet Journal, Bareback Alchemy, the Darwin Murders* and *Stories from a Holiday Heart* anthologies and Saint Julian Press. He is also a web Shorty Award nominee, a contributing editor for Wikipedia and a frequent guest speaker on live, radio interview broadcasts.

In 2012, he was the Massachusetts Project Organizer for the global "100 Thousand Poets for Change" for which he received a signed letter of commendation from Governor, Deval Patrick. This world-wide event became the largest, single poetry reading in the history of the world and was archived by Stanford University.

Cambria Jones was born in Minneapolis, MN, and currently resides outside the Twin Cities. She dabbles in history and writing, always enjoying a good cup of coffee and people watching. She is new to the publication arena, but eagerly anticipates upcoming features in *The Wayfarer, Stone Path Review, The Penman Review,* and *Mezzo Cammin*.

Lois P. Jones is host of "Poet's Café" (KPFK, Los Angeles 90.7 fm), and co-produces the Moonday poetry reading series at The Little Theater in Santa Monica, California with Alice Pero. She is the Poetry Editor of *Kyoto Journal* and a multiple Pushcart nominee. She has work forthcoming in *Eyewear* and has published in *Narrative Magazine, American Poetry Journal, The Nassau Review, Qarrtsiluni, Sierra Nevada Review, Askew, Raven Chronicles, The Warwick Review* and other journals in the U.S. and abroad. Lois's poems have won honors under judges Kwame Dawes and Fiona Sampson among others. New Yorker staff writer, Dana Goodyear selected "Ouija" as Poem of the Year in the 2010 competition sponsored by IBPC. She is the winner of the 2012 Tiferet Poetry Prize and the 2012 Liakoura Prize and is featured in *The Tiferet Talk Interviews* (2013), which includes transcriptions of interviews conducted by host Melissa Studdard and guests Robert Pinsky, Ed Hirsch, Julia Cameron and others.

Allison Joseph lives, writes, teaches and runs in Carbondale, Illinois, where she is on the faculty of Southern Illinois University. Her latest books are *My Father's Kites* (Steel Toe Press) and *Trace Particles* (Backbone Press). She recently received the Paladin Award from *Rhino*

Magazine.

Winnie Khaw is a creative writing MFA candidate at Mills College. Her work is featured in *Magic Lantern Review, Empty Mirror Books, Passages North, Palooka Journal, The Philadelphia Review, Eclectica, The Daily Satire*, etc. She was waitlisted for the 2013 Lit Camp conference in San Francisco, and was Chapman University's nominee for the Association of Writers award in fiction in 2011.

Lissa Kiernan's first book, *Two Faint Lines in the Violet* (Negative Capability Press, 2014) explores poetry's unique ability to document yet re-vision the nuclear age, how when singing somewhere between the personal and political—if we listen closely—we might hear the social. Kiernan holds her MFA from the Stonecoast program at the University of Southern Maine and an MA in Media Studies from The New School for Social Research. She is the founding director of The Rooster Moans Poetry Cooperative, a leading provider of MFA-caliber online poetry education.

Robert S. King, a native Georgian, now lives in the mountains near Hayesville, NC. His poems have appeared in hundreds of magazines, including *California Quarterly, Chariton Review, Hollins Critic, Kenyon Review, Lullwater Review, Main Street Rag, Midwest Quarterly, Negative Capability, Southern Poetry Review,* and *Spoon River Poetry Review*. He has published four chapbooks (*When Stars Fall Down as Snow,* Garland Press 1976; *Dream of the Electric Eel,* Wolfsong Publications 1982; *The Traveller's Tale,* Whistle Press 1998; and *Diary of the Last Person on Earth,* Sybaritic Press, 2014). His full-length collections are *The Hunted River* and *The Gravedigger's Roots,* both in 2nd editions from FutureCycle Press, 2012; and *One Man's Profit* from Sweatshoppe Publications, 2013. Another collection, *Developing a Photograph of God,* is available from Glass Lyre Press.

Usha Kishore is an Indian born British poet, writer and translator. Usha now lives on the Isle of Man, UK, where she teaches English in a Secondary School. Usha's poetry is internationally published and anthologized by Macmillan UK, Hodder Wayland UK, Oxford University Press (UK) and Harper Collins India, among others. Usha was the winner of the Pre Raphaelite Poetry Prize (UK) in October 2013. Her work has been part of many international projects and is part of the British Primaryand Indian Middle School syllabus. The winner of an Isle of Man Arts Council Award and a Manx Heritage Foundation Award, Usha's debut collection On Manannan's Isle is forthcoming from dpdotcom, UK in February 2014. A book of translations from the Sanskrit, *Translations of the Divine Woman* is also forthcoming from Rasala Books, India in 2014.

Among other places, **Laurie Kolp's** poems have appeared in *PoetsArtists, MiPOesias, Writer's Digest, The FIB Review, cho (Contemporary Haibun Online), The Crafty Poet: A Portable Workshop* by Diane Lockward; and are forthcoming in *Blue Fifth Review*. Laurie's first poetry collection, *Upon the Blue Couch*, is set for release March 2014 through Winter Goose Publications.

Victoria Korth is a poet and psychiatrist living in upstate New York. She holds a Master's Degree in Creative Writing at the State University of New York, Brockport. Her thesis, *Tender Warnings: Narrative Tension in Lyric Poetry*, explores the relationship between narrative elements in her own life, biography revealed to her through her work as a physician and the lyric impulse. Recent poems have appeared in the *Spoon River Poetry Review, Worcester Review, Passager, Barrow Street, 2013 Longlist Anthology: Montreal International Poetry Prize*, and elsewhere.

W.F. Lantry, native of San Diego, received his Maîtrise from L'Université de Nice, and PhD in Creative Writing from University of Houston. His poetry collections are *The Structure of Desire* (Little Red Tree 2012), winner of a 2013 Nautilus Award in Poetry, *The Language of Birds* (Finishing Line 2011), a lyric retelling of Attar's *Conference of the Birds*, and a forthcoming collection *The Book of Maps*. Recent honors: the Hackney Literary Award in Poetry, Lindberg Foundation International Poetry for Peace Prize (in Israel), and *Potomac Review* Prize. His work appears in *Atlanta Review, Asian Cha* and *Aesthetica*. He currently works in Washington, DC and is an associate fiction editor at *JMWW*.

Rustin Larson's poetry has appeared in *The New Yorker, The Iowa Review, North American Review, Poetry East, Saranac Review, Poets & Artists* and other magazines. He is the author of *The Wine-Dark House* (Blue Light Press, 2009) and *Crazy Star* (selected for the Loess Hills Book's Poetry

Series in 2005). Larson won 1st Editor's Prize from *Rhino* magazine in 2000 and has won prizes for his poetry from The National Poet Hunt and The Chester H. Jones Foundation, among others. A seven-time Pushcart nominee, and graduate of the Vermont College MFA in Writing, Larson was an Iowa Poet at The Des Moines National Poetry Festival in 2002 & 2004, a featured writer in the DMACC Celebration of the Literary Arts in 2007 & 2008, and he was a featured poet at the Poetry at Round Top [Texas] Festival in May 2012. His latest collection, *Bum Cantos, Winter Jazz, & The Collected Discography of Morning*, won the 2013 Blue Light Book Award (Blue Light Press, San Francisco).

Ann Neuser Lederer was born in Ohio and has also lived and worked in Pennsylvania, Michigan, and Kentucky. Her poems and creative nonfiction appear in journals, anthologies such as *Bedside Guide, Best of the Net*, and *The Country Doctor Revisited*; and chapbooks *Approaching Freeze, The Undifferentiated,* and *Weaning the Babies.* Additional information is available at https://sites.google.com/site/annneuserlederer/. She is employed as a nurse in Kentucky.

Stephen Linsteadt is a painter, poet, and writer. He is the founder of Scalar Heart Connection and author of the book with the same title. He has published articles about metaphysics and consciousness in *Whole Life Times, Creations Magazine*, and others. His poetry is published in *Moments of the Soul* (Spirit First), *Solstice, Cradle Songs* (Quill and Parchment Press), *Saint Julian Press, Poets on Site*, and others. His paintings have appeared in *Reed Magazine, Badlands Literary Journal, Birmingham Arts Journal, Woman in Metaphor*, and can be seen at StephenLinsteadtStudio.com.

Dennis Maloney is the editor and publisher of the widely respected White Pine Press in Buffalo, NY which will celebrate its 40th year in 2013. He is also a poet and translator. His works of translation include: *The Stones of Chile* by Pablo Neruda, *The Landscape of Castile* by Antonio Machado, *Between the Floating Mist:Poems of Ryokan,*and *The Poet and the Sea* by Juan Ramon Jimenez.

A number of volumes of his own poetry have been published including *The Map Is Not the Territory: Poems & Translations* and *Just Enough*. His book of Yosano Akiko translations, *Tangled Hair*, was published in 2012 by Palisades Press.

Alexandra Martin grew up in the Los Angeles area and currently lives in Pasadena, CA, where she works for A Room of Her Own Foundation to support creative women. She received her BA in Religious Studies from Stanford University and is currently pursuing her MFA in Poetry at the Vermont College of Fine Arts. In her spare time, she runs, attempts yoga, drinks copious amounts of coffee, and searches for the peacocks that roam wild in Pasadena.

Matt McGee writes poetry and short fiction in the local library until the staff makes him go home. His recent collection, *We Liked You Better When You Was a Whore*, is available on Amazon.

Ken Meisel is a poet and psychotherapist from the Detroit area. He is the author of five books of poetry, the most recent being *Scrap Metal Mantra Poems*, a finalist in the *Main Street Rag* Chapbook Contest, published in 2013 and *Beautiful Rust*, [Bottom Dog Press: 2009]. He is a 2012 Kresge Arts Literary Fellow and a Pushcart Prize nominee. He has had poems published in *Cream City Review, Rattle, San Pedro River Review, Boxcar Review, Birdfeast, Chaffin Journal* and *Concho River Review*.

B.Z. Niditch is a poet, playwright, fiction writer and teacher. His work is widely published in journals and magazines throughout the world, including *Columbia: A Magazine of Poetry and Art; The Literary Review; Denver Quarterly; Hawaii Review; Le Guepard (*France*); Kadmos (*France*); Prism International; Jejune (*Czech Republic*); Leopold Bloom (*Budapest*); Antioch Review;* and *Prairie Schooner,* among others. He lives in Brookline, Massachusetts.

Richard King Perkins II is a state-sponsored advocate for residents in long-term care facilities. He has a wife, Vickie, and a daughter, Sage. He is a two-time Pushcart nominee and his work has appeared in hundreds of publications including *Poetry Salzburg Review, Prime Mincer, Sheepshead Review, Sierra Nevada Review, The William and Mary Review, Two Thirds North,* and *The Red Cedar Review.* He has poems forthcoming in *Bluestem, Emrys Journal,* and *December Magazine.*

Anne Elezabeth Pluto was born in the Bronx and grew up in Brooklyn. She is Professor of Literature and Theatre at Lesley University in Cambridge, MA where she is the artistic director of the Oxford Street Players. She was a member of the Boston small press scene in the late 1980's and the editor of *Oak Square Magazine.* She started *Commonthought Magazine* at Lesley 24 years ago. Her chapbook, *The Frog Princess*, was published by White Pine Press. She has been a participant at the Bread Loaf Writers' Conference in 2005 and 2006. Her most recent publication is *Lubbock Electric*, available from the U.K.'s Argotist Editions. She lives in Boston with her family.

Brie Quartin recently hit the 20th anniversary of her 30th birthday and decided she wanted a redo. She allowed herself a few contemplative moments to take stock in passions long forgotten and vowed that most of her next 50 years would be spent doing things that bring her joy and fill her bucket. And so began her re-acquaintance with poetry, which in some odd way was like finding an essential piece to her life that she hadn't realized was missing. She has been published previously in the *Freshwater Poetry Journal* as a poetry contest winner judged by CT Poet Laureate Dick Allen, as well as work submitted for general submission.

Cindy Rinne creates art and writes in San Bernardino, CA. She is the Poetry Editor for the *Sand Canyon Review*, Crafton Hills College, CA. Cindy is a Guest Author for *Saint Julian Press*. She is a founding member of PoetrIE, an Inland Empire based literary community. Her work appeared or is forthcoming in *Phantom Kangaroo, Lyre, Lyre, Cactus Heart Press, The Wayfarer, Twelve Winters Press, The Lake, Revolution House, Soundings Review, East Jasmine Review, Linden Ave. Literary Journal,* and others. She has a poetry manuscript, *The Feather Ladder*, and has written and illustrated a chapbook called, *Rootlessness.* www.fiberverse.com.

Mary Kay Rummel is the first Poet Laureate of Ventura County, CA. Her seventh book of poetry, *The Lifeline Trembles*, is being published by Blue Light Press of San Francisco as a co-winner of the 2014 Blue Light Poetry Prize. She teaches part time at California State University, Channel Islands and divides her time between Ventura and Minneapolis.

Peter L. Scacco is the author of the poetry chapbooks *Poems along a Path*, *A Quiet Place*, and *Chiaroscuro*. His poems and woodcuts have been featured in a variety of print and online publications. Mr. Scacco has lived and worked in New York, Paris, Tokyo, and Brussels, and he now resides in Austin, Texas. His art can be seen at www.scaccowoodcuts.com.

LeRoy N. Sorenson began writing when he was a teenager: essays, commentary pieces, short stories and poetry. He has worked as a child psychologist, political organizer, and financial analyst. He was one of four poetry participants in the 2009-2010 Loft Mentor Series at the Loft Literary Center in Minneapolis, MN, and a semi-finalist for the Pablo Neruda Prize for Poetry. He currently is a participant in the Loft's Foreword program. He lives in St. Paul, MN.

Ron Starbuck is the author of *When Angels Are Born* and *Wheels Turning Inward*, two rich collections of over fifty poems, following a poet's mythic and spiritual journey that crosses easily onto the paths of many contemplative traditions. He has been intensely engaged in an Interfaith-Buddhist-Christian dialogue for many years. Ron holds a lifelong interest in Christian mysticism, comparative religion, theology, and various forms of contemplative practice. He is also the Publisher-CEO of Saint Julian Press, Inc.; forming an independent literary press to work with emerging and established writers and poets, and tendering new introductions to the world at large in the framework of an interfaith and cross cultural literary dialogue has been a long time dream. He has written for *Parabola Magazine* and authors an Interconnections blog on the *Saint Julian Press* website.

Donna Baier Stein's writings appear in *Virginia Quarterly Review, Prairie Schooner, Puerto del Sol, Washingtonian*, and many other journals and anthologies. Her story collection *Great Drawing Board of the Sky* was a Finalist in the Iowa Fiction Awards and will be published in December 2013 as *Sympathetic People*; her novel *The Silver Baron's Wife* received the

PEN/New England Discovery Award and is seeking representation. She was a Founding Poetry Editor of *Bellevue Literary Review* and currently publishes *Tiferet: A Journal of Spiritual Literature*. Awards include a scholarship from *Bread Loaf*, fellowships from Johns Hopkins University and the New Jersey Council for the Arts, awards from the Poetry Societies of Virginia and New Hampshire, an Honorable Mention from the Allen E. Ginsberg Poetry Prizes, four Pushcart nominations and prizes from *Kansas Quarterly, Florida Review*, and elsewhere. In 2012 she received a scholarship from the Summer Literary Seminars and her poetry chapbook *Sometimes You Sense the Difference* was published by Finishing Line Press. www.donnabaierstein.com

Robert Strickland is a poet, composer, singer, and multi-instrumentalist. His family hails from the American Deep South, with English and Dutch roots. Splitting his time between Colorado and Florida, he pursues his interest in the intersection of poetry, music, photography, painting and other art forms. His work has appeared in a number of publications, including *Burning Word Literary Journal, Pale River Review, Red Poppy Review, Toucan, Poetry Breakfast*, and *Houseboat*, where he was a featured poet.

Melissa Studdard is the author of *My Yehidah, The Tiferet Talk Interviews*, and the bestselling novel, *Six Weeks to Yehidah*, and her first poetry collection, *I Ate the Cosmos for Breakfast*, is forthcoming this fall. Her books have received numerous awards, including the Forward National Literature Award, the International Book Award, January Magazine's best children's books of the year, The Reader's Favorite Award, and the Pinnacle Book Achievement Award. She serves as a reviewer-at-large for *The National Poetry Review*, a professor for Lone Star College System and host of *Tiferet Talk* radio.

Tim Suermondt is the author of two full-length collections: *Trying to Help the Elephant Man Dance* (The Backwaters Press, 2007) and *Just Beautiful* from New York Quarterly Books, 2010. He has published poems in *Poetry, The Georgia Review, Blackbird, Able Muse, Prairie Schooner, PANK, Bellevue Literary Review, Stand Magazine (U.K.)*, and has poems forthcoming in *Taos Journal of Poetry and Art, Plume Poetry Journal* and *North Dakota Quarterly*, among others. After many years in Queens and Brooklyn, he has moved to Cambridge with his wife, the poet Pui Ying Wong.

Maria Terrone is the author of three poetry collections: *Eye to Eye* (Bordighera Press, 2014); *A Secret Room in Fall*, co-winner of the McGovern Prize from Ashland Poetry Press; and *The Bodies We Were Loaned*, plus a chapbook, *American Gothic, Take 2*. Her poems, nominated four times for a Pushcart Prize, have appeared in such magazines as *Ploughshares, The Hudson Review,* and *Poetry,* and in 20 anthologies. In 2012 she wrote a 20-minute narrative, "At Home in the New World, that was commissioned by the Guggenheim Museum and performed in Queens. Visit her at www.mariaterrone.com

Born and raised in Charleston, S.C., moved to Chicago, educated at red-bricked universities and on city streets, **Charles Thielman** has enjoyed working as a social worker, truck driver, city bus driver and enthused bookstore clerk. Married on a Kauai beach, a loving Grandfather for five free spirits, his work as Poet and shareholder in an independent Bookstore's collective continues! A video of his reading at Tsunami Books can be found at http://www.youtube.com/watch?v=d-5-G_jaoJY. And not a few of his other poems have been accepted by literary journals, such as *The Pedestal, Gargoyle, Poetry365, The Criterion* [India], *Poetry Salzburg* [Austria], *Gangway, Windfall* [Oregon], *Muse* [India], *Battered Suitcase, Poetry Kanto* [Japan], *Open Road, Poetry Kit* and *Pastiche* [England], *Belle Reve, Tiger's Eye* and *Rusty Nail*.

Angela Narciso Torres' first book of poetry, *Blood Orange*, won the 2013 Willow Books Literature Award for Poetry. Recent work appears in *Cimarron Review, Colorado Review,* and *Cream City Review*. A graduate of Warren Wilson MFA Program for Writers and the Harvard Graduate School of Education, Angela has received fellowships from the Illinois Arts Council, Ragdale Foundation, and Midwest Writing Center. Born in Brooklyn and raised in Manila, she currently resides in Chicago, where she teaches poetry workshops and serves as a senior poetry editor for *RHINO*. www.angelanarcisotorres.com

Jon Tribble is the Managing Editor of the literary journal *Crab Orchard Review* and is the Series Editor of the Crab Orchard Series in Poetry from SIU Press. He has published poems in print journals, including *Ploughshares, Poetry, Crazyhorse, Quarterly West, Brilliant Corners, The Southeast Review, Black Zinnias, Sycamore Review, Whetstone, Alaska Quarterly Review, Southern Indiana Review,* and *South Dakota Review*;

online, including in *Caper Literary Journal, Prime Mincer Literary Journal, A River & Sound Review, Prime Number, Contemporary American Voices: A Journal of Poetry, A Poetry Congeries at Connotation Press: An Online Artifact, storySouth,* and *The Account: A Journal of Poetry, Prose, and Thought;* and in several anthologies. He was the recipient of the 2001 Campbell Corner Poetry Prize and he received a 2003 Illinois Arts Council Fellowship in Poetry.

Kenneth Weene's poetry has appeared in numerous publications – most recently featured in *Sol* and publication in *Spirits,* and *Vox Poetica.* An anthology of Ken's writings, *Songs for my Father,* was published by Inkwell Productions in 2002. His short stories have appeared in many places, including *Legendary, Sex and Murder Magazine, The New Flesh Magazine,* and *The Santa Fe Literary Review.* Ken's novels, *Widow's Walk, Memoirs From the Asylum,* and *Tales From the Dew Drop Inne* are published by All Things That Matter Press. http://www.authorkenweene.comLawrence College. He lives in Carbondale, Illinois, and teaches at Southern Illinois University.

Helen Wickes worked for many years as a psychotherapist and received an MFA from the Bennington Writing Seminars in 2002. Glass Lyre Press published her second and third books—*The Moon Over Zabriskie* and *Dowser's Apprentice*—in 2014. Sixteen Rivers Press will publish *The World As You Left It* in 2015.

Pui Ying Wong was born in Hong Kong. She is the author of a full length book of poetry *Yellow Plum Season* (New York Quarterly Books, 2010), two chapbooks: *Mementos* (Finishing Line Press, 2007), *Sonnet for a New Country* (Pudding House Press, 2008) and her poems have appeared in *Crannog (*Ireland*), Gargoyle, Prairie Schooner, The Southampton Review, Ucity Review,* and *Valparaiso Poetry Review* among others. Her work has been nominated for the Pushcart Prize, Best of the Web and she was a finalist for the 2011 Sundress Best of the Net editions. She lives in Cambridge with her husband, the poet Tim Suermondt.

Saint Julian Press, Inc.
Houston

Saint Julian Press as a literary and educational organization embraces a vision to create a local and worldwide community, by engaging in a literary and artistic dialogue to promote world peace, cultural conversations, and an interfaith awareness, appreciation, and acceptance.

In our mission as a literary press we wish to encourage, nurture, and share transformative literature and art of both past and living masters. While giving new and emerging artists, poets, and writers a place they may come home to and share their work.

Our inspiration is Julian of Norwich, the 14th Century English mystic and anchoress, who scholars believe was the first woman to write a book in the English language. Her major work, the Sixteen Revelations of Divine Love, touches at the heart of our mission.

Our hope is to publish transformative literature and art that symbolizes a radical openness to the literary and visual arts, cultures, and faiths across humanity. Opening far and wide the doors to a cultural dialogue and exchange; creating a global community that cultivates meaningful and transforming conversations that cross cultures, secular societies, and encourage an interfaith exchange.

Saint Julian Press

Poetry Collection

I Ate the Cosmos for Breakfast
Melissa Studdard
When Angels Are Born
Ron Starbuck
Wounded Bud
Fred LaMotte

www.saintjulianpress.com

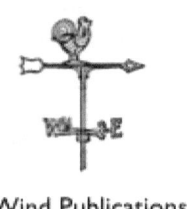

Wind Publications

A poetry tutorial to inform and inspire poets. Includes model poems and prompts, writing tips, and interviews with poets. Geared for experienced poets as well as those just getting started. Ideal for individual use at home or group use in the classroom or workshop.

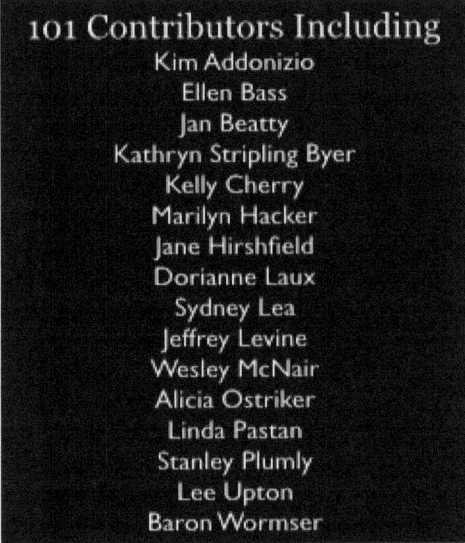

101 Contributors Including
Kim Addonizio
Ellen Bass
Jan Beatty
Kathryn Stripling Byer
Kelly Cherry
Marilyn Hacker
Jane Hirshfield
Dorianne Laux
Sydney Lea
Jeffrey Levine
Wesley McNair
Alicia Ostriker
Linda Pastan
Stanley Plumly
Lee Upton
Baron Wormser

... an important new resource for poets—those who are just beginning as well as the more seasoned poet.—Susan Rich

... a spectacular array of model poems and information from poets on how they see the craft. It will get you writing and will keep you writing.—Sheila Bender

... a *must* for teachers of poetry...What a way to ease our students into finding their own toolboxes.—Grace Cavalieri

---

Wind Publications, 600 Overbrook Drive, Nicholasville, KY 40356
ISBN: 978-1936138623   Price: $20
www.windpub.com   books@windpub.com
Available at Amazon, B&N, or your favorite bookstore

When Angels Are Born

by

Ron Starbuck

When Angels Are Born celebrates poetry as a language of deep intimacy, a language meant to touch the human spirit and awaken it to the mystery of life, all life. These poems are an invitation into a world that is intimate and wondrous, one that explores the depths of all human hearts. Beckoning the reader to engage in a spiritual practice of divine intimacy that opens the eyes and ears of the human heart, and invites a person into the mystery of relationships and creation, a world of openness and timelessness.

Such a practice offers the reader an opportunity to explore the mystery of human thought, interconnections, creativity, and design, our deepest intentions, in a perichoresis or divine dance of words, love, intimacy, and transformation. Through this dance and practice, this openness the reader may discover a spiritual indwelling, an intimacy, where we discover oneness at work throughout creation, where we find that we dwell within one another, come and dance this divine dance. "That they all may be one; as thou, Father, art in me, and I in thee, that they also may be one in us (John 17:21)."

Ron Starbuck is my kind of poet - he writes with a clarity and simplicity that draw me into feelings and images that can never be clear and simple. His angels can be seen everywhere, but they speak of mystery that can never be captured anywhere. My favorite among his angels is his dog, "Nick," his "old friend" who "taught me the truth of unconditional love." ~ Paul F. Knitter, Paul Tillich Professor of Theology, World Religions, and Culture, Union Theological Seminary, New York, and author of Without Buddha I Could not be a Christian.

Ron Starbuck makes his poems from a very particular point of inflection, reflection and at times of deep genuflection. There are moments of lyrical beauty, of human intimacy shared with the stranger-reader that elevate the personal into the universal. There are also insights born of deep experience and transmuted into words and rhythm that gently and powerfully invoke the sense of the sacred. This marriage of emotion and spiritual consciousness makes this poetry especially memorable and helpful to the quest for the personal knowledge of truth that his readers will be urged more eagerly to make as they become more familiar with his voice and vision. ~ Laurence Freeman OSB, author of First Sight: The Experience of Faith, and Jesus The Teacher Within.

www.saintjulianpress.com

the FutureCycle Poetry Book Prize & honorarium

2014 CONTENDERS
Jane Blue
Randy Blythe
Christopher Bursk
J.P. Dancing Bear
Diane Furtney
William Greenway
Paul Hostovsky
Joseph Hutchison
Stephen Longfellow
Melanie McCabe
Lee Passarella
Tim Peeler
Elizabeth Schultz
Leon Weinmann
Gerald Yelle

Visit us for info, catalog, and submission guidelines

FutureCycle Press
futurecycle.org

"100 Proof"
Editing, Proofreading, and Typing Services

REASONABLE RATES
PERSONAL ATTENTION

CIN HOCHMAN
President

poet2680@aol.com

New Books by Joan Colby

SELECTED POEMS (FutureCycle Press)
PROPERTIES OF MATTER (Aldrich Press)
BITTERSWEET (Main Street Rag Press)
Available from Amazon.com or Main Street Rag Bookstore.
JoanMC@aol.com
www.joancolby.com

Naugatuck River Review
*a journal of narrative poetry *
in print semi-annually
Lori Desrosiers, Editor
Subscriptions and Guidelines:
http://naugatuckriverreview.com

the Selected Poems *series*

Our Selected Poems series highlights contemporary poets with a substantial body of published work to their credit. Our goal is to resurrect superb but often out-of-print poems.

the Good Works *projects*

Our Good Works projects are thematic anthologies of individual works devoted to significant issues affecting our world. All proceeds from sales are donated to charities.

Visit us for info, catalog, and submission guidelines

Free Kindle Saturdays and countdown deals

Check our Catalog tab each Saturday

FutureCycle Press
futurecycle.org

Monthly Goodreads Giveaways

Book excerpts in our Goodreads group

Live Lyre
Reading Series

Presented By

Glass Lyre Press

Exceptional works to replenish the spirit
www.GlassLyrePress.com

GLASS LYRE PRESS, LLC
"Exceptional works to replenish the spirit"

Poetry collections
Poetry chapbooks
Select short & flash fiction
Anthologies

Glass Lyre Press is an independent literary publisher interested in technically accomplished, stylistically distinct, and original work. Glass Lyre seeks diverse writers that possess a dynamic aesthetic, and an ability to emotionally and intellectually engage a wide audience of readers.

Glass Lyre's vision is to connect the world through language and art. We hope to expand the scope of poetry and short fiction for the general reader through exceptionally well-written books, which evoke emotion, provide insight, and resonate with the human spirit.

www.GlassLyrePress.com

MIDWESTERN GOTHIC
A LITERARY JOURNAL

Midwestern Gothic aims to collect the very best in Midwestern fiction writing a way that has never been done before, cataloging the oeuvre of an often ove looked region of the United States ripe with its own mythologies and tall tales.

$12 PRINT
$2.99 EBOO

SUBSCRIPTION
1 YEAR / 4 ISSUE
$40 PRINT / $10 EBOC

MIDWESTGOTHIC.COM

www.ingramcontent.com/pod-product-compliance
Lightning Source LLC
Chambersburg PA
CBHW030308080526
44584CB00012B/490